Killer
Athletes

America's Elite
Special Operations Warriors
Share Lessons & Advice
To
Help Athletes Become Champions!

AUTHOR'S NOTE

No classified information was used in the preparation of this book. All of the material contained within this book is derived from unclassified sources. The names of certain individuals cited in this book have been altered to protect their true identities. The views and opinions expressed in this book do not necessarily reflect those of the entire special operations community, military and sports medicine, the Department of Defense or all of the individuals cited or otherwise mentioned.

This book offers fitness, nutritional, mental toughness and other types of self-improvement related information and is designed for educational purposes only. The information contained in this book may not be appropriate for all individuals, and you should not consider this information as a substitute for, nor does it replace professional medical advice, diagnosis, or treatment. You should always consult a physician before starting or modifying any diet or exercise program.

Table of Contents

Introduction

Chapter 1: Special Operations

Chapter 2: The Warriors

Chapter 3: Special Operator Traits and Habits

Chapter 4: The Special Operator's Mindset

Chapter 5: Killer Athletes

Chapter 6: Character

Chapter 7: Nutrition

Chapter 8: Physical Training

Chapter 9: Hydration

Chapter 10: Heart Rate

Chapter 11: Rest and Recovery

Chapter 12: Practice

Chapter 13: Dealing with Distractions

Chapter 14: Dealing with Injuries

Chapter 15: Mental Toughness

Chapter 16: Fear and Stress

Chapter 17: Breathing Technique

Chapter 18: Thinking without Limits

Chapter 19: Before the Battle Begins

Chapter 20: Setting Goals

Chapter 21: It's Time for Action

Introduction

This book has been in the works for many years. I have had it rattling around in the back of my mind as I have gone from one place to another, and from a young man to a - shall we say - *"more mature and seasoned"* one. I have had the privilege, throughout a long military career, of knowing and serving with members of almost every Special Operations unit in the armed forces of the United States. While interacting with these men over the course of many years, our informal conversations would inevitably delve into our personal lives and what we'd done prior to entering the military. I found that most of these men had participated in various individual and team sports at the youth, high school and collegiate levels. Most were average athletes, some had achieved state-wide success, and still others were skilled enough to become scholarship athletes at the college level. Some had actually achieved national-level success in their respective sports, achieving varying degrees of recognition in some of the more prestigious national tournaments and competitions. A few of them had even competed at the international level as members of U.S. national teams.

Whatever level of sport these men had participated in, all of them, without exception, felt that their experiences as athletes helped them successfully prepare for and complete the difficult selection process required of their respective special operations unit. These men also believed that many of the lessons they had learned as young athletes also helped them perform well throughout their subsequent service in operational units. This in itself is not remarkable; for centuries participation in sports has been used as a vehicle for the physical and mental development of warriors. The earliest Olympic Games were focused almost entirely on events such as wrestling, boxing, running, throwing a spear for distance and accuracy, all of which had direct application to warfare as it was conducted at that time.

Throughout the years, in many of the personal conversations I had with these warriors we exchanged our experiences in the various sports we had participated in. One particular question that I always inserted into the conversation was:

> *"What if we could go back in time, knowing what we now know about mental toughness, performing under pressure and training methodologies, and begin our athletic careers all over again?"*

In almost every instance, the men in the room would fall silent as they reflected on this question.

Once the conversation resumed, it became obvious that everyone agreed on one point: Had they, as young athletes, known just a fraction of what they now knew, their approach and attitude toward their specific sport would have been much different; and they probably would have achieved a much higher degree of success as athletes. The men were now seasoned veterans of some of America's premier military units, and all felt that the knowledge, experience and perspective they had acquired during their time in special operations units would have been incredibly valuable to them while they were developing physically and mentally as young athletes.

During the past several years, it has become a common practice for athletic directors and coaches to have members of special operations units speak to their teams at the beginning of the season or before a significant event or competition. Some special operations units actually conduct events for sports teams that focus on team-building, leadership, mental toughness and other character traits and individual skills. Unfortunately, most young athletes never get the opportunity to attend one of these events or speak with members of special operations units.

This book was written specifically for these young men and women. It will serve as a vehicle for the transfer of some of the knowledge and perspective possessed by these highly-experienced warriors to young athletes, their parents and their coaches. The information and lessons contained in it can help an athlete quickly gain an edge as a competitor and it can also be of great benefit from an overall personal development perspective. While aimed primarily at young athletes currently participating in various sports, this book can help anyone desiring to enhance various aspects of their personal and professional lives.

Special Operations

This book is based, essentially, on the sharing of knowledge gained from the experiences of very highly qualified special operators. Through the knowledge being shared, you will become aware of some of the individual traits, philosophies and experiences of members of America's elite Special Operations Forces. I believe it is important that you gain an appreciation for the special operations community in general, and the individuals that are assigned to these units and are tasked with executing difficult missions in every region of the world.

The various units that comprise America's Special Operations Forces (SOF) are unique because they provide the United States with a broad range of military capabilities. While their specific missions, areas of focus and expertise are often quite different, all SOF units share one very critical requirement: The necessity for individuals of high character, who possess unique abilities that enable them to achieve success in high-pressure and dangerous situations in which most other men would likely fail.

To better understand what SOF units are trained to do, one must understand the meaning of *special operations*. The following is the definition of *special operations* as defined in military manuals used by U.S. Armed Forces:

Special Operations – Actions conducted by specially organized, trained, and equipped military and paramilitary forces to achieve military, political, economic, or psychological objectives by non-conventional military means in hostile, denied, or politically sensitive areas. They are conducted in peace, conflict, and war, independently or in coordination with operations of conventional forces.

Political-military considerations frequently shape special operations, requiring clandestine, covert, or low-visibility techniques and oversight at the national level. Special operations differ from conventional operations in terms of the degree of physical and political risk, operational techniques, mode of employment, their independence from friendly support, and dependence upon detailed operational intelligence and indigenous assets.

Special operations are different from conventional military operations in that they often require sustained independent actions and operations in situations, circumstances, or environments beyond those that regular military forces are equipped and trained to handle. The selection and training processes combined with specialized skills and capabilities distinguish SOF units from conventional military units.

Special Operations Missions

All SOF units are trained to perform missions that fall into one of five main categories:

Unconventional Warfare (UW) – Activities conducted to enable a resistance movement or insurgency to coerce, disrupt, or overthrow a government or occupying power by operating through or with an underground, auxiliary, or guerrilla force in a denied area. UW operations include a broad spectrum of military and paramilitary operations, normally of long duration. They are predominantly conducted through, with, or by indigenous or surrogate forces that are organized, trained, equipped, supported, and directed by an external source to varying degrees. These operations include, but are not limited to, guerrilla warfare, subversion, sabotage, intelligence activities, and unconventional assisted recovery.

Foreign Internal Defense (FID) – Activities taken by a foreign government's civilian and military agencies in order to assist another government or designated organization to free and protect its society from subversion, lawlessness, insurgency, terrorism, and other threats to its security. The primary intent is to help the legitimate governing body to address internal threats and the underlying causes of these threats. During recent combat operations in Iraq and Afghanistan, members of various SOF units assisted in the organization and training of host-nation military and paramilitary forces.

Direct Action (DA) – Activities that include short-duration strikes and other small-scale offensive actions conducted as special operations in hostile, denied, or politically sensitive environments, which employ specialized military capabilities to seize, destroy, capture, exploit, recover, or damage designated targets. DA operations may include raids, ambushes, and assault tactics (including close-quarters battle); the emplacement of mines and other munitions; executing standoff attacks by fire from air, ground, or maritime platforms; providing terminal guidance for precision-guided munitions; conducting independent sabotage and anti-ship operations; or recovering or capturing personnel or materials. DA operations are often associated with the pursuit of objectives of great strategic importance, such as the Navy SEAL operation in May of 2011 that resulted in the death of the notorious terrorist Osama bin Laden.

Counterterrorism (CT) – Activities taken directly against terrorist networks; and indirectly to influence and render global environments inhospitable to terrorist networks. CT operations may be conducted in environments that are denied to conventional forces because of political situations or threatening conditions.

Special Reconnaissance (SR) – Activities that are conducted in the pursuit of information deemed to be of strategic or operational significance. SR operations may be conducted using various overt and covert techniques and tactics.

It is not uncommon for various aspects of two or more of these missions to be executed simultaneously during a special operation. It is an understatement to say that the individuals who are tasked with the execution of these missions require high levels of training and skill.

SOF units typically:

- Require candidates to successfully complete very demanding selection processes that are designed to identify men capable of performing well in extreme conditions or situations. Once admitted to a SOF unit, special operators receive mission-specific education and training that greatly exceeds that which is associated with conventional military forces.

- Maintain a high level of competency in more than one military specialty. (Selected SOF units are regionally oriented for employment; cross cultural communication skills are a routine part of training.)

- Operate in a clandestine manner to ensure mission success.

- Maintain a very high level of pre-conflict readiness, and are often in the first echelon of any commitment of U.S. Forces.

The Special Operator

For simplicity's sake, throughout this book I will refer to the men assigned to the various SOF units as *special operators* or *operators.*

Several stereotypes regarding physical appearance have been assigned to special operators throughout the years. Although many of them are in fact impressively built, many of them are also of average physical appearance; not heavily muscled or of extraordinary height or physique.

Likewise, some are inclined to think that members of SOF units are all brawn and no brain. In other words, they believe that special operators are of somewhat average intelligence and require constantly being told what to do, how to do it and where to do it. Nothing could be further from the truth! Sadly, this *"dumb killer"* image has probably been perpetuated by the portrayal of special operators on Hollywood productions or by other facets of the media.

Actually, members of special operations units, in general, must possess high levels of intelligence and the ability to think critically in very intense situations. While an operator's physical ability is obviously very important, it is his intelligence and ability to think clearly under great stress that is most valued by the leaders of SOF units.

Based on information made public by the leadership of the U.S. Special Operations Command, here are some characteristics of the typical special operator:

- Is married and has at least two kids

- Average age is 29 years-old enlisted; 34 years-old officer

- Has 8 years of experience in the conventional forces

- Receives cultural and language training

- Has attended multiple advanced tactical schools

- Enjoys games which require problem solving like chess

- Is well educated and likely to have a college degree

- Is a thinking athlete - water polo, track, wrestling, lacrosse, or football

Role Models not Idols

The very purpose of this book is to enable you to leverage some of the knowledge, perspective and techniques used by special operators as you strive to attain your athletic goals. However, it is important for you to remember that while men who have successfully completed an incredibly demanding SOF selection course, and went on to serve as special operators, should be respected and in many ways admired; you should not view them as perfect human beings. It is quite common for non-military people to be so impressed by the mystique surrounding current or former special operators that they tend to develop a form of *"idol worship"* that causes them to cling to every word these individuals say during interviews or write in their books or on their blogs or websites.

Any honest special operator will freely admit that passing a selection course and serving in a SOF unit does not in itself mean that a person is automatically suited to be an effective role model or mentor. Special operators are not immune to personal issues and problems experienced by many other people, and some of them (a very small percentage) have actually run afoul of the law by committing serious crimes.

Don't misunderstand what I am trying to convey, the vast majority of the members of SOF units are truly exceptional people and worthy of your respect and admiration. But, like any other population or group of people, SOF units also have their *"ten-percenters;"* those individuals who, for various reasons or in some ways, might not be the type of person you should seek to emulate. With this knowledge in mind, you can now keep a balanced perspective as you learn more about the mindset and other attributes that enable special operators to routinely achieve what many would consider impossible.

Conventional Military Forces

This book is obviously focused on sharing the experiences and advice of members of various SOF units. I want to ensure that readers understand that while they are rarely mentioned in this book, the non-SOF units in America's armed forces, which are typically referred to as *conventional forces*, are not to be considered in any way inferior or unworthy of your attention. Special operators do not have a monopoly on courage, mental toughness and proficiency in battle. There are very few, if any, major conflicts or combat operations of significant scope and duration that can be successfully executed by SOF units or conventional forces acting on their own. The skillful synchronization of the efforts of both types of forces is what enables America's military to project combat power world-wide; it is a total team effort and one that is based upon mutual respect and an awareness of how each unit or member of the team contributes to the accomplishment of the mission.

I'll end this chapter by sharing the thoughts of a retired special operator that served in SOF units for more than three decades. He said:

"During the many years I've worked with special operators, I was always somewhat amazed by how normal and ordinary these men appeared to be. They were not levitating several inches above the ground nor did they typically possess anything from a physical appearance perspective that would make them stand out in a crowd.

They often had many of the same problems that most people have as they experience life; issues with their spouses, children, financial difficulties, strained relationships with peers and seniors at work, etc. They all stumbled and fell at times when facing challenges and situations and they often struggled with various levels of frustrations regarding their personal and professional lives. In fact, on the outside, their lives appeared pretty much the same as those of most people.

What made these men different was inside of them; it was their character and unbending will to succeed. They had learned how to push forward when their emotions and bodies urged them to quit. They had developed what I call 'unbeatable minds,' *and men with such minds are impossible to defeat. They can be killed or injured to the point that they are physically incapacitated, but as long as these men can breathe, inside their minds they are trying to figure out a way to win. That's the* 'secret weapon' *these men possess."*

The Warriors

I believe it is important for readers to have a basic understanding of how the concept of the individual warrior developed over time and exists still today in America's SOF units and other elite military units around the world. This chapter is designed to provide this information, admittedly, on a very broad scale and in relatively few words. It is critical that you understand that the special operators that provided the material for this book live their lives as warriors in every aspect. It is this way of life that produces the mindset, philosophies and attitudes that enables them to routinely operate effectively in dangerous situations that, in my opinion, can be utilized by athletes of all ages as they pursue their individual dreams and goals.

The Warrior Class

Centuries ago, due to the constant conflicts occurring throughout history, many nations and societies developed what was known as the *"warrior class."* The warrior class – a group of men recognized for their skill in combat or waging war - was often the dominant factor in determining whether a nation, society or tribe survived or was eliminated from the face of the earth. As such, the warrior class was afforded great respect by royalty and the common citizenry, and the individual warrior was celebrated as being the ideal example of what all young males should aspire to become.

By the end of the 19th century, the concept of a warrior class or *"military caste"* had largely become an anachronism in most modern nations. Though the term *"warrior"* was still sometimes used, it was typically in reference to members of large, organized professional armies and naval forces comprised of civilians who were either conscripts or volunteers. These men left civilian life, served in the military forces for a period of time and then returned to civilian life to become members of society at large. In the ancient context, being a member of a warrior class meant that one was literally born into a class or caste of people whose sole purpose in life was to become a *"man of arms"* and serve the nation as a soldier – for life.

America's Warrior Class

Since the birth of America, our nation's armed forces have evolved from militias and small, relatively untrained organizations, to very large, highly trained and capable instruments of war that have no equal in today's world. Many of the professional soldiers that serve in today's armed forces consider themselves to be part of America's warrior class, in the best sense of the term. I believe that the vast majority of members of special operations units not only feel that they are part of this country's warrior class, but that they are truly the elite of the elite!

Although it is rarely, if ever, discussed among special operators, I think that most share the belief that they are the modern day equivalent of the Spartan warrior, Greek Hoplite, Roman Centurion and other notable warriors of ancient times. It is important that you are aware of and understand that this mindset and the approach to living the life of a warrior are what make these men special. If you leverage this knowledge properly and appropriately, it can help you transform yourself from just another athlete to a warrior that competes with a will to win that very few of your peers and competitors will ever achieve.

The Rite of Passage

Throughout history, elite military units have had exceptionally demanding tests, or *rites of passage,* to determine if young males were worthy of becoming a warrior. The Spartans had the Agoge – the crucible into which all young males were thrust and, if survived, were transformed into warriors worthy of representing Sparta. The Agoge was designed to make Spartan boys grow into fierce warriors and to instill in them patriotism, loyalty, obedience and comradeship. America's special operations units all have their own unique rite of passage which is used to identify candidates capable of serving as a special operator.

It is important that you fully understand a couple of terms and definitions that will be used throughout this book. Within the special operations community, the terms *training* and *selection* have two very distinct and different meanings.

A *training course* is one in which students are educated and trained in specific concepts, skills and techniques. For example, an Army Ranger attending a sniper course will learn the tactics and techniques associated with serving as a sniper. Likewise, a member of an Air Force Pararescue unit that attends a course on high-altitude life-saving techniques will be exposed to information and knowledge specific to that type of mountainous environment. As you can see, a training course is all about learning and the acquisition of new skills or the refinement or enhancement of existing skills.

A *selection course* is one that is designed to screen, test and evaluate students for certain physical and mental attributes that have been deemed critical by the leaders of specific SOF units. The major difference between a selection course and a training course is that selection is all about identifying the men that possess these qualities and allowing them to gain admission to the unit. Obviously, those that are found lacking relative to these attributes and qualities will be removed from the course.

While each of the selection courses currently being utilized by the various SOF units are somewhat different in content and duration, they share a common theme of putting young men into situations of intense physical and mental stress, typically induced by nearly continuous physical exercise, reduced sleep and constant evaluation by instructors.

In his book, "*Always Faithful, Always Forward: The Forging of a Special Operations Marine,*" retired Navy SEAL Dick Couch had this to say about the rites of passage associated with America's special operations community:

> *"Few processes in our culture, military or otherwise, lay bare the physical, psychological, and emotional worth of an individual as do our SOF selection programs. It is a rendering for the essentials of the human spirit."*

All of these very demanding selection courses require candidates to exhibit great amounts of mental toughness, determination, resilience and the ability to think and act appropriately during stressful situations. It is these qualities and traits that are essentially the focus of this book, in the hope that young athletes can leverage some of the lessons learned by these special operators in order to elevate their own mindset in relation to their sport.

The Warrior

Commonly accepted definitions for the term warrior are: "*a person who fights in battles and is known for having courage and skill*" and "*one who is engaged aggressively or energetically in an activity, cause, or conflict.*"

Obviously, the members of special operations units can be described as warriors and they, like the great warriors of ancient times, are completely committed mentally and physically to their cause.

A special operations warrior is someone that willingly places the best interests of his country and of his teammates above his own desires, preferences or goals. You may recognize some commonality between the mindset and attitude demonstrated by special operators and many highly successful athletes. Clearly, much of what makes a man a successful special operator applies to individuals that are high-achievers in their chosen sport.

The Warrior's Code

Throughout history, warriors have been guided by certain principles and philosophies that were developed over time. It is interesting to note that since ancient times, these warrior codes almost always contained some common core principles, ideals or values. Even more telling is that these fundamental concepts can be found in many facets of modern life such as military units, academia, business and athletics. As you read more about them, you'll undoubtedly recognize some or all and realize that these concepts are essentially what your parents, coaches and mentors have been emphasizing to you since you were a very young child. You'll also learn how special operators apply these concepts and how you can use them to enhance your character, and ultimately, your performance as an athlete.

Listed below are some of the common core traits found in some of the warriors codes used in the past and present times:

Honor

Honor is a concept that is based upon an individual's personal integrity. Honor is a matter of carrying out, acting, and living the values and ethos that guide the members of one's unit or team. It's found in one's beliefs, but exhibited through one's actions. Acting with honor is not only a duty, but also a distinction, as those who possess honor are held in honor by their teammates. Simply stated, it is honor that guides those who do the right thing when no one is watching.

Loyalty

All members of the military swear an oath that they will bear true faith and allegiance to the United States Constitution. Implied in this oath is that they will also be loyal to their specific branch of the armed forces, their units and their fellow warriors. Bearing true faith and allegiance is a matter of believing in and devoting yourself to something or someone. In the special operations community, loyalty means that an operator will do everything he can to support his leaders and his teammates in any situation, including those that are associated with extreme danger and the possibility of injury and loss of life.

Discipline

Discipline is the hallmark of the individual special operator, and it is the trait that enables him to constantly seek improvement in his mind and body as he prepares for the time when he will be tested in battle. Discipline is what enables a special operator to willingly sacrifice many aspects of his personal life in order to pursue excellence in the mental and physical skills that can literally save his life and those of his teammates during combat situations. It is discipline that causes a special operator to endure constant training and to develop the ability to perform in a consistently excellent manner. All of this applies to athletes as well, as they seek to attain a high-level of skill and success in their specific sport.

Knowledge

Special operators possess specialized knowledge and skills that are acquired by rigorous and continuous education, training and practical experience. All of this produces individual warriors and units that possess capabilities that greatly exceed those of conventional soldiers and organizations. While this knowledge and advanced skills are themselves impressive, the real value is the ability these men possess to effectively apply them when it matters most – in the heat of battle. Likewise, high-level athletes also possess a level of knowledge and skills that exceed most of their competitors, but it is their ability to utilize these capabilities at the crucial time that separates the winners from the losers.

Strength

Strength is an obvious requirement for special operators, and it is developed from both a physical and mental perspective. Experience has shown that the most important factor associated with the success of a special operator is his strength of mind or *mindset*. Without this, the physical strength and attributes an operator may possess will ultimately prove less effective and in some instances, ineffective. You've probably already seen examples of this in your sport; instances in which very talented and skilled athletes have everything it takes to win, yet fail to perform well due to something that is lacking from a mental perspective. When we talk about strength in this context, we are really talking about a person's character, which in turn is the foundation upon which everything else is built. Strength of character, the type that special operators are known for, is created through a conscious and continuous pursuit of excellence. In subsequent chapters, we will discuss the development of character in great detail. Likewise, we will also learn more about physical training and the development of a strong body.

Courage

Courage is an attribute that most people associate with members of special operations units. Many people believe that special operators do not experience fear as a result of their extensive training. This is not true, these warriors are not immune to fear – their brains, like those of all humans, were hard-wired through evolution to recognize dangerous or threatening situations and in turn produce fear, anxiety and other emotions or reactions that can have a negative impact on their performance. Experienced special operators are very effective at controlling the effects of fear, and this is what enables them to act courageously and decisively in situations that might cause other men to retreat and seek safety. Being courageous is also essential for high-level athletes, as is controlling the physical and mental effects of fear. Both of these topics will be covered in detail in subsequent chapters.

Although the traits listed above are the essence of what makes up the warrior ethos that is common to all special operators, these men must also demonstrate a passion for learning and continuous improvement. In order to be a truly exemplary athlete and perform at optimal levels, it is crucial that you adopt this philosophy of being a *"lifelong learner."* Thirst for knowledge, combined with a never-ending quest for excellence are two of the main characteristics that fuel the actions of special operators and champion athletes alike!

Special Operator Traits and Habits

The nature of the missions that Special Operations Forces execute demands a unique type of individual. It is imperative that the men who will eventually carry out these missions possess some specific traits and habits that will enable them to respond appropriately to threats, sudden changes, set-backs and unforeseen events. Although some of these attributes are related to physical fitness and endurance, most of them actually have to do with an individual's character, work ethic and strength of will. You'll quickly realize that these traits and habits are also essential to your success as an athlete, and as such, you should continuously seek to develop and improve them.

Character: The warriors of the special operations community routinely operate in remote regions of the world executing missions that are vital to the strategic interests of the United States. The stakes are often quite high, and in some instances the success or failure of these warriors will have a rapid and significant impact upon how America is viewed by the rest of the world. These operations are often conducted in a clandestine manner, which isolates these units and deprives them of the types of support normally available to conventional military units. All of this means that the members of these units have to rely on each other for the successful accomplishment of the mission, and in many instances, their very survival.

The bottom line is that when the chips are down and bullets are zipping through the air, these men have to count on each other to do what is necessary to win. In situations like this, the one thing that enables a man to disregard danger and take action is his character, and this is precisely why the special operations community places so much emphasis on this personal attribute and demands that every special operator has demonstrated he possesses it.

Character is also an essential ingredient for success at the highest levels of sport, and for the most part, the most revered champions in your sport, when examined closely, will be shown to be of strong character. This topic will be covered in detail in a subsequent chapter. For now, reflect on the fact that this attribute – character – is the very first trait listed in this chapter devoted to the traits and habits found in successful special operators. Suffice it to say that character is the foundation upon which all else is developed in special operators and athletes alike.

Self-Discipline: All special operators possess high-levels of self-discipline. I think it is fair to say that almost all of them possessed this trait prior to joining the military and that it enabled them to gain entrance to the special operations community. Self-discipline, in my opinion, is at the root of all that a person accomplishes or fails to accomplish during his life. It drives him or her to acquire additional knowledge and skills and to avoid anything that will detract from his goal of always being at the top of his game. Self-discipline is the force behind sound choices and deliberate actions that lead to positive outcomes. It allows special operators and athletes alike to withstand extreme levels of physical pain and emotional stress while pursuing their goals and it also enables them to understand their limitations at times when it is essential to do so.

Mental Toughness: Mental toughness is a core attribute of every special operator. Without it, it would be impossible for a man to successfully complete any of the selection courses associated with all U.S. special operations forces. Mental toughness also plays a major factor in the battlefield success during extremely dangerous combat operations. There are certain factors that comprise mental toughness, and this topic will be covered in detail in the Mental Toughness chapter.

Resilience: Special operators have to be resilient, whether engaged in training or actual combat operations. Challenges, conditions and situations will vary, but all are best handled by a highly trained warrior possessing an inner strength that enables him to prevail over whatever is facing him at the moment. These warriors routinely face situations in which it would seem logical for them to abort a mission or retreat in the face of unexpected enemy threats or events. During these situations, they tap into a reservoir of resolve and resilience developed through hard training, which enables them to endure and achieve when most men would simply quit.

Special operators must demonstrate resilience and the ability to adapt to rapidly changing battlefield situations. These warriors do encounter setbacks – things don't always go as planned, especially in combat. Plans go awry, weather conditions change unexpectedly, helicopters break down or even crash, radios fail at critical moments and in some instances, their teammates are killed or wounded. Training and inner strength is what enables operators to quickly recover during situations like these, assess the status of their plan and adapt it appropriately to accomplish the mission.

The bottom line is that operators must be hard men with the ability to *"get the job done"*, no matter what it takes. For this reason these men expect much of themselves, and hold themselves and each other accountable to a standard in which the only acceptable outcome is success – accomplishing the mission. Athletes must also be capable of absorbing adversity, rolling with the punches, and rapidly rebounding with actions that will result in victory.

Goal Mindedness: The typical special operator is a very goal-oriented person and in most instances, they probably demonstrated this trait at an early age. Many of these men set high personal and professional goals for themselves as early as their middle-school or high school years. I've met many special operators that told me they had decided to become a member of a SOF unit at a very young age, and devoted much of their youth doing things that would help them achieve this goal.

Most high-achievers in any profession maintain a list of personal and professional goals, which are often segmented into short-term, mid-term and long-term categories. In this book, you'll see references to the competitive nature of the men that are associated with the special operations community. It is important to know that in many instances, these men are competing against themselves as they pursue their dreams. This is a habit that everyone who wishes to improve in their personal and professional lives can create, and it is especially helpful for athletes that aspire to maximize their potential in a specific sport. You can start by working on setting some simple goals that you know you can easily accomplish and then move on to more complex, longer-term ones.

The main point is that in order to achieve great things as an athlete you must define some specific goals to help you focus your time and behavior. Everything you do should be done with a purpose or goal in mind – an *"end state"* that must be attained in order to declare *"mission accomplished."* The old military adage, *"If you fail to plan, you are planning to fail"* certainly applies to young athletes!

Proactivity: Like most high-achievers, special operators are typically forward-looking individuals that demonstrate a very proactive approach to every aspect of their lives. They are capable of independent thought and, most importantly, they are self-starters with a habit of assessing what actions need to be considered or taken to achieve success. Special operators are often faced with situations that require decisiveness and rapid action. During situations such as these, they know that they cannot afford to sit and wait and see what happens. Their training has developed in them a bias for action. Experienced operators are very aware of what they can control or affect and what they cannot. Rather than waste time worrying or complaining about things that are outside of their control, they focus on what they can affect – and they plan and execute actions that are likely to lead to favorable results. In other words, these warriors know that it is almost always better to be proactive than reactive. They know from experience that when forced to be reactive, they often are not in control of a situation and this can lead to undesirable situations or events, especially during combat operations. Obviously, the mentality of being proactive and having a bias for action has great utility in the world of sports and your success as an athlete.

Planning: It should be obvious that much of the success achieved by special operations units is a direct result of the precise execution of strategies, plans, and tactics. Every attempt is made to control as many factors as possible when devising courses of action that will lead to the successful completion of a mission or assigned task. When time permits, special operators engage in very detailed planning for missions and operations, utilizing all of their experience and skills to produce a game plan that stacks the deck in their favor as it pertains to the successful accomplishment of the assigned mission. This is made possible by utilizing the collection of many years of operational experience that have been consolidated into various standard operating procedures (SOPs). Theses SOPs cover a myriad of tasks, tactics, and techniques that an operator will be required to execute in training or during combat operations; they are memorized and drilled relentlessly by every member of the unit. The goal is flawless and seamless execution, regardless of conditions on the battlefield. You probably recognize this concept from your own experience as an athlete. You should realize that when your coaches require you to learn and repeatedly execute specific game plans or situational drills, they are very much aligned with what elite military units do to achieve excellence and maximize the chances for success.

Expectation of Success: The members of special operations forces are supremely confident and they expect to win. Aside from the superb tactical and technical training they receive, they are taught to use visualization techniques prior to engaging in a challenging event or operation. The use of visualization techniques is relatively new to special operations units. While there are differences in some of the visualization methods used by these units, all are generally focused on visualization and rehearsal of specific actions that will -or may need to be- performed during a mission. During visualization sessions, operators see themselves performing the various steps, procedures, techniques, and tactics that will be required to successfully complete the mission. For example, a Navy SEAL will visualize the actions he will have to take to exit a submerged submarine in total darkness and proceed toward a designated target area on land. Another example is when members of a Ranger unit will mentally walk through the steps associated with fast-roping from a helicopter onto the roof of a building so they can provide supporting fires for an assault element from another SOF unit that is entering an adjacent structure in pursuit of a targeted enemy combatant. The lesson here is that regardless of whatever physical and mental preparation special operators do prior to executing an operation, they have at their core a mentality of winning – of successfully completing the mission. These men, like the best athletes in the world, expect to win every time they approach the battlefield!

Readiness for the Unexpected: Typically, the operations conducted by SOF units are very well planned, to include detailed timelines, phases of execution and synchronization with other U.S. and allied units. Despite this, it is quite common for unexpected situations to arise that require the operators on the ground to make rapid and in some instances, significant changes to the plan. Much of what happens during these situations is described as the Fog of War, a term which will be covered in a subsequent chapter. Knowing that these situations will occur, the leaders of SOF units have established various methods of training that enables special operators to develop exceptional levels of mental agility and decisiveness during times of extreme stress and confusion. During countless training exercises, these men are subjected to situations full of uncertainty and chaos that require critical thinking and decision-making.

The result is an individual operator that is able to quickly assess the situation on the battlefield and make rapid and appropriate decisions that lead to the successful accomplishment of the mission. As demonstrated by seasoned special operators, a person's ability to cope with pressure and unforeseen circumstances is a skill that can be acquired and perfected. It is a skill that is highly valuable in almost all sports and one which you'd be wise to learn more about.

Continuous Learning: Based on the typical portrayal of special operators in the movies, books and other forms of media, I think many people view these warriors as unintelligent brutes. This is simply not true. While often impressive from a physical appearance perspective, these men are all highly intelligent. In fact, while the various SOF selection courses are all associated with rigorous physical challenges that require great strength and endurance from trainees, daily life in a SOF unit places much more value on a man's mind than on his ability to run or swim fast.

Today's special operators utilize some of the most highly sophisticated equipment used by any military force in the world. Because of today's high-tech weaponry, satellite communications gear, laser-optics and an ever-increasing number of technical devices and tools that help them maintain an edge on the battlefield; these warriors must be highly intelligent, fast learners. The leaders of SOF units also place great emphasis on continuous research on the latest technologies and tools available that can help their organizations to remain relevant in today's ever-changing battlefield.

Every tenured special operator (those that spent their entire career in a SOF unit) I have ever known, continuously pursued additional knowledge in some aspect of warfare during their off-duty time. Some really loved weaponry, so they became experts on all aspects of combat shooting. Their interest in such things enabled them to assist in the development of new and improved sniper rifles and associated gear. In the 70's and 80s, small groups of trainers from SOF units learned close quarter battle (CQB) skills and lessons from more experienced law enforcement agencies, SWAT teams of major American cities and some highly regarded foreign counter-terrorist units. Likewise, much energy has always been devoted to the study of emerging technologies and how they can be applied to special operations.

It should not surprise you that, like special operators, most highly-successful athletes also utilize the lifelong learner philosophy to surpass the competition. You should do some reflection on this point and ask yourself if you are doing everything possible to actually increase your knowledge relative to various aspects of your sport. At the highest levels of athletic competition, victory almost always results from the intelligent and timely application of tactics and techniques. Are you doing your best to enhance your knowledge and skills?

In order to reach your goals and become a champion athlete, it will require a lot of work, determination and discipline. Throughout this book you will be presented with the tools you need in order to develop yourself and grow as an athlete. If you are open to and willing to apply the concepts contained in this book, and are ready to put in the effort and work tirelessly, I am confident that you will succeed in maximizing your athletic potential.

The Special Operator's Mindset

In addition to the various attributes mentioned in previous chapters, special operators also share some common attitudes and philosophies that collectively form what I refer to as the *special operator's mindset*. This mindset results in warriors that are mentally agile and able to adapt to rapidly changing circumstances. A critical component of the special operator's mindset is the practice of focusing their energy and effort on factors that they can control, and not to waste time worrying about factors that are beyond their control. This simple concept is often overlooked by many athletes and I think it should be studied and embraced by those seeking to elevate their performance.

As portrayed in movies, war often appears as a relatively straight-forward and simple concept. In reality, because of the many factors and conditions that can be found on the battlefield, conducting combat operations often becomes quite difficult. These factors and conditions are collectively referred to as *friction*, which Baron Carl Von Clausewitz, a famous 18th century Prussian general described as being *"the force that makes the apparently easy so difficult."* In warfare, as in sports, friction is the force that makes the seemingly easy things difficult and the difficult things impossible!

War is essentially a clash of opposing wills, with each military force trying to resist the other's actions while simultaneously trying to impose its own will on the enemy. These opposing forces are not inanimate objects, rather, they are both independent units led by humans making decisions. In such an environment, friction abounds. I think it is rather obvious that the world of sports also shares this dynamic, albeit with far less at stake for the loser!

Friction

In general, there are two types of friction, internal and external, that can affect the outcome of a military operation, athletic contest and practically everything else a person does or attempts to do in life. This is a simple concept to understand, yet for many, it is quite difficult to master: Properly managing friction before, during and after an important event or challenging situation. As you read about the two types of friction, reflect upon the presence of either in your personal life and your role as an athlete.

Internal Friction: This type of friction, also referred to as *self-imposed friction*, consists of those elements that combatants have some level of control over. During combat operations, friction may be mental, such as inability to decide what course of action to take, or reacting too slowly to rapidly changing circumstances on the battlefield. This internal friction can be the result of personality clashes, defective leadership, a lack of coordination or communication, poor planning, inadequate training, lack of proper mental or physical preparation and many other things that are generally controllable, to some extent, by the combatants. In other words, the way to *control* these internal frictions is to do your due diligence *prior* to the event; then you won't be plagued with self-doubt at a crucial moment.

External Friction: This type of friction consists of those things that combatants have little or no control over. Examples include actions taken by the enemy force, physical obstacles (natural or man-made), the terrain the battle is being fought on and the weather. Each of these is typically beyond the control of any soldier, including special operators, and they can have a very serious and often, negative impact upon a unit's plan of attack.

An Air Force Special Operator's Thoughts on Friction

I spoke with a very experienced member of an Air Force special operations unit about the effects of friction during combat operations and asked him to provide some of his thoughts on the topic. He said:

> *"Your examples of internal and external friction are spot-on; both types of friction can be found in almost everything my unit does, whether it is during training or while on real-*

world ops. Our experience has enabled us, through honest and detailed self-assessment of our team members and our actions, to pinpoint most of the areas in which internal friction can exist. To be honest, we found that most of our internal friction issues were associated with personality clashes and inadequate communication between the unit leaders and the guys at the tip of the spear, so to speak. We've done a lot of work to ensure that our leaders and team members are on the same frequency regarding the objectives and plan of attack throughout all phases of an operation. We have done a lot to eliminate the inevitable personality clashes that can arise when you have so many strong-willed 'Type-A' personalities operating with each other.

If you look at various professional sports teams, many of them seem to be dominated by or overly focused on the personality or talent of one or perhaps just a few of the players. Many of these teams end up having problems due to this. In our unit, we do our best to eliminate the 'prima donna' or 'superstar' mentality that might exist; it simply isn't tolerated. When it comes to external friction, we've just come to accept that it will exist despite our best intelligence and planning efforts, and that like any other SOF unit, our success will always depend on our operators being able to think on their feet and make the right decisions when things happen that make our game plan unworkable. To sum it up, we do everything possible from an individual and unit perspective to minimize instances of internal friction and we train relentlessly to enhance our ability to successfully cope with every imaginable type of external friction."

In sports, friction of either type that is not controlled or negated will inevitably result in a negative psychological and physical impact on athletes. Thus, every attempt should be made to minimize internal or self-imposed friction in order to focus on being able to perform in whatever external friction exists before and during actual competition. Identifying and minimizing sources of internal friction is relatively simple. By developing and applying the previously mentioned traits, habits and techniques that are possessed and utilized by special operators, you will be able to better control your behaviors, reactions and therefore minimize the negative impact that internal friction can have on you.

Being able to effectively cope with external friction - that which arises from factors outside of your control - is not as easy to accomplish. This takes determination and strength of mind and spirit. When it comes to actually operating or performing in situations associated with high levels of external friction, athletes actually have an advantage that special operators do not often possess. At every level of athletics, there will be actual competition against an individual opponent or team, depending on the specific sport. During competitions, athletes are exposed to the typical forms of friction associated with their sport, such as the physical layout of the venue, the size of the audience, range of skill levels of your opponents, etc.

In other words, athletes have the ability to *"go to war"* on a fairly continuous basis to not only practice the execution of their specific skills, but to repeatedly expose themselves to the friction and stresses associated with live competition. Special operators do not have this advantage. Despite the outstanding training they receive, the fact is that the friction of their arena – the battlefield – cannot be fully replicated in a safe environment. For these warriors, the friction associated with their *"game day"* – actual combat operations - brings about the very real possibility of death and serious injury!

If you reflect on this, you will begin to realize that, although many aspects of the external friction associated with your sport are beyond your control, you can actually enhance your ability to handle it by frequently participating in actual competitive events. Adopting the mindset of focusing your efforts on those things which you can control, and not wasting any time worrying about the things you can't, can have a huge impact upon your performance as an athlete.

Factors You Cannot Control

Genetics: One of the most obvious factors you cannot control when it comes to being an athlete is your genetics. While the human body can be made stronger and faster by undergoing specific training, it is impossible to influence height, skeletal structure, length of limbs, size of hands, etc. The good news is that members of special operations units and Olympic champions alike come in all shapes and sizes, which means that, while *ideal* physical or athletic attributes do exist in most sports, history has proven that many athletes excel and reach the highest levels of their sports despite lacking these attributes.

Teammates: While most special operators typically don't have any control over who is allowed to join their respective units, they do know that all of their teammates have successfully passed the same selection and testing they went through. This provides them with the confidence in the knowledge that all of their teammates have at least some things in common, especially in the areas of dedication, desire to be a member of the team, etc. For the most part, as an athlete, you cannot control who your teammates are, nor can you control how much enthusiasm they have for your specific sport or their level of dedication and commitment to training and achieving success. During your athletic career, you will probably have teammates that do not share your attitude, motivation and goals. This is something you should expect and be able to cope with, so it doesn't have a negative impact on your performance as an athlete.

Coaches: Members of SOF units know that their leaders have *"been there, done that"* regarding special operations, they know these men are competent and have earned the privilege of serving in a leadership role.

Individual special operators also trust their leaders to have the best interests of the unit and its members as their highest priority. Unfortunately, the same cannot be said about some individuals serving as coaches for sports teams. Athletes typically have no control over who their coaches are, how competent they are or their attitudes toward their athletes. Assuming that most coaches are sincere individuals with a genuine desire to help their athletes excel, there is still the very real possibility that many of them simply lack the experience and knowledge to be a highly effective coach. Once again, as an athlete, you probably cannot choose who the coach of your team will be, and you must expect that at some point, one or more of your coaches may be lacking in some aspect and that you'll need to be ready to find a way to overcome this situation.

The Battlefield: Special operators have to train and be ready to conduct operations in every type of climate and terrain. They usually have no say in choosing what environments they will operate in. Suffice it to say that special operators never have the home field advantage! Knowing this, they train in every part of the world, learning valuable lessons that are specific to each region, climate, etc. While you probably won't have much control over where you'll be competing as an athlete, you do have the advantage of knowing, in most instances, where your events, games or matches will be conducted. This will enable you to visit the selected venue and get acquainted with the playing surface, the layout of the area, where the fans will be, etc.

Factors You Can Control

Knowledge and Technique: Special operations and sports are quite similar in that both have existed for centuries and require a great amount of specific knowledge, lessons, tactics and techniques. One of the most common characteristic shared by special operators is their insatiable thirst for knowledge, which they attempt to satisfy by continuous study of topics associated with the *Profession of Arms*. Of the many special operators that I've had the honor of knowing and working with, the vast majority of them spent a great amount of their personal time studying and learning. They focused much of their studies on other successful military units and high-achieving individuals and attempted to assess what they had done or were doing that made them the best at what they did.

In today's world of digital technology and various forms of media, special operators and athletes alike have relatively easy access to countless videos, books, reports and studies, interviews and other content associated with the experts in any discipline or sport. Aside from what your coaches can teach you (remember, some coaches are simply more capable than others), you have total control over how much of your own time you will spend seeking knowledge from other sources. In addition to the many sport-specific developmental clubs and camps that exist in many cities and towns, almost every sport in America now has internet-based video portals or membership sites (free or fee-based) that offer access to instruction by high-level coaches and athletes.

Proficiency and Skill Level: It is one thing to possess knowledge of tactics and techniques associated with your sport; it is quite another to actually be proficient at employing or executing the same with a high degree of skill. For example, the members of special operations units assigned to assault teams that routinely enter and clear enemy-occupied buildings, all learned a great amount about various weapons, tactics and techniques associated with what is typically referred to as *close-quarter battle* (CQB) operations. But, knowledge alone does not produce the level of shooting accuracy required of a special operator. Only after expending literally thousands of rounds of ammunition during countless CQB practice sessions, does a special operator earn the most basic designation as qualified member of an assault team. After they've earned this basic qualification, they typically are assigned to a permanent unit, where they will undergo much more training at an even higher level that brings their CQB skills to a world-class level.

As previously mentioned, today's athletes have unprecedented access to a great amount of sport-specific knowledge and technique. But, like special operators new to CQB operations, only a significant amount of well-planned, focused and deliberate practice will result in an athlete becoming proficient at executing new skills and techniques during actual competition. The amount of practice you devote toward improving your proficiency and skills is entirely under your control. Obviously, young athletes also have to attend school and maintain proper focus on their academics, but aside from this and perhaps any duties or chores they have to perform as a member of their family, they usually have a great amount of time available each day. What these young men and women choose to do with their time is obviously up to them, but I don't think anyone will disagree with my assertion that athletes that utilize some of their free time to study and practice various aspects of their sport will almost always attain more success than peers and competitors that choose not to do so.

Nutrition: Unlike special operators serving in remote regions of the world who may have to eat highly-processed combat rations or even local food of varying quality, you will generally have the ability to control everything you eat and drink while training and competing. Obviously, nutrition plays a large factor in athletic performance and you should exercise control over this aspect of your life to the greatest extent possible. This topic is discussed in greater detail in the Nutrition chapter.

Conditioning: You've already learned that your genetics were predetermined at the moment you were conceived in your mother's womb. You cannot train your body to grow another two inches in height, grow longer arms or a larger or smaller skeletal frame. The good news is that you have total control over your level of physical conditioning and this can help you overcome some of the *"genetic deficiencies"* you may have been born with. Special operations units are full of guys that when measured against the *ideal operator profile* are too short, too tall, too small, too heavy or run too slow. What this means is that a high-level of conditioning combined with similar levels of determination, mental toughness and confidence can enable a person to achieve things that others say are unattainable or even impossible. Everyone reading this book has the opportunity to become the most highly-conditioned athlete on their team!

Rest and Recovery: Members of special operations units typically live fast-paced and often, somewhat hectic and unpredictable lives. It is not unusual for these men to be away from home for over 85% of each year. While away training or participating in combat operations, they often have to operate without proper rest and recovery, which often leads to physical injuries, diminished performance and mental fatigue. On the other hand, as an athlete, you have a great amount of control over the amount of rest you get and how long your recovery periods will be between training sessions or competitive events. The athletic community has learned much over the past twenty years or so about the importance of adequate rest and recovery and you can benefit from this knowledge if you choose to do so. We'll cover this topic in greater detail in the Rest and Recovery chapter.

This chapter has introduced you to some important concepts that are heavily utilized by members of special operations units, and which you can leverage as an athlete. The ability to understand the two types of friction and how they can affect your performance, as well as the philosophy of *"controlling what you can, and not wasting time on things beyond your control"* are both of vital importance to you as an athlete. Integrating these concepts into your competitive mindset is a must if you aspire to break through to the next level as an athlete. I recommend that you do some reflection on the material in this chapter and look for ways that you can begin to put it to immediate use!

Killer Athletes

The warriors of America's special operations community do not seek to merely compete with their enemies, but to dominate them to the point of completely overwhelming and killing them. To some, this may sound a bit cruel or even barbaric, but it is the truth; the battlefield is often associated with conditions and actions that most people would consider savage or uncivilized. In such situations, competing is simply not good enough. Those who walk onto the battlefield to compete typically end up dying; however those who come to dominate are the ones that survive, often bloodied and battered, but alive – and victorious! Over time, those that have faced America's elite warriors in combat have learned that these men are formidable foes, and that they fight with a tenacity that is intimidating and deadly at the same time.

One unique aspect of America's special operations community is the presence of this attitude of *"domination versus competition."* Everyone associated with this elite community operates with a mindset of *"maxing out"* and strives to achieve excellence in all that they do. This mindset is developed through various forms of exceptionally challenging training, most of which has a competitive aspect associated with it. Over time, men that came from all walks of life are transformed into fierce warriors that possess high levels of mental toughness, self-discipline, and resilience. They also demonstrate a relentless will to win that is often described as the Killer Instinct: The ability to ruthlessly and quickly exploit an opportunity or weakness shown by the enemy, and to overcome any obstacles that may appear between them and victory. These men do not simply expect success - they demand it, and their actions ensure that it happens more often than not.

Now, you may be thinking that what you've just read is somewhat harsh; after all, athletes in any sport are not trying to kill their opponents! However, the requirement for athletes desiring to reach the highest levels of their sport, to develop this same type of killer instinct is very real. Often, when two athletes of comparable talent, experience, physical ability and technical skills are engaged in a high-stakes and pressure-packed competition, victory is determined by which of them has the tenacity and sheer force of will that gives him or her the courage to seize opportunities at critical moments.

Such athletes develop a reputation for having a seemingly innate ability that repeatedly enables them to *"find a way to win"* when the odds are stacked against them. Like their special operations counterparts, these men and women often become the *"opponent that nobody wants to fight."* They become what I refer to as Killer Athletes, the fierce and courageous individuals that more often than not are standing at the top on the awards podium when the competition is over, receiving the gold medals and other accolades that are given to champions.

I am quite sure that everyone reading this book knows of one or more *Killer Athletes* in their particular sport. These are men and women that have developed reputations for being fierce and relentless opponents; many athletes literally dread competing against them because they know they are in for the fight of their lives. I also believe that most, if not all, of the readers of this book would like to become known as a Killer Athlete, for all of the right reasons and to enjoy the many benefits, tangible and intangible, that are associated with being such a feared and respected warrior.

The subsequent chapters of this book will share some of the lessons, philosophies, concepts and techniques that have helped America's elite warriors elevate their physical and mental capabilities to exceptionally high levels. The material you are about to read has been shaped by the wisdom and experiences of these battle-hardened special operators, all of whom were once competitive athletes. The insights and perspective shared by these men can be of great benefit to any athlete that is seeking to not merely compete, but to dominate!

Character

The nature of special operations missions often place extraordinary physical and psychological demands on the members of SOF units. It is no secret that the men conducting these missions are often operating deep inside enemy-controlled or otherwise unfriendly territory without the comforting presence of allied units that can be relied upon to quickly come to their aid if necessary. It takes a specific type of person to volunteer to serve in a role which will frequently require him to operate in some of the most remote and dangerous regions in the world. It's an understatement to say that when small teams of special operators are executing some of the most dangerous missions one can imagine, each special operator literally places his safety and survival in the hands of his teammates. This quintessential 'spirit' exhibited by members of these units can be summarized in one word: character.

The fact that this book contains an entire chapter devoted to this topic should serve as an indicator of the importance personal character holds in the eyes of members of the special operations community; and how critical your own character will be to your ultimate success as an athlete.

What Is Character?

The famous Greek philosopher, Aristotle, taught his students that the ultimate aim of human life and activity is development of character. He believed that the most notable achievement a man could attain during his life was to become known as a Man of Character, and to continuously exhibit all of the qualities and virtues associated with this term.

John Wooden is considered by many to be the most successful basketball coach in NCAA history. His teams at UCLA won ten national championships in a 12-year period, including an unprecedented seven consecutive titles. As famous as he was for his teams' success on the basketball court, he ultimately became even more highly-regarded for the mentorship he lent to his players as well as the relentless emphasis he placed on their character development. Seen below are two quotes attributed to Coach Wooden on the topic of character:

> *"The true test of a man's character is what he does when no one is watching."*

~~~

> *"Be more concerned with your character than your reputation, because your character is what you really are, while your reputation is merely what others think you are."*

> *– John Wooden*

The Importance of Character in Special Operations

Much has been written about the various physical and military skills associated with serving as a member of a SOF unit. Impressive as these qualities may be, they are quite useless if the men possessing them are not first and foremost Men of Character. Character in the context of special operations is essentially the unequivocal knowledge that no matter how insurmountable the odds, how precarious the mission, how hopeless the situation, a special operator will always be willing to do whatever is necessary – often even knowingly face the probability of death – to accomplish a mission.

In a special operations unit every single member has to be able to be counted on and depended on when times get tough. Every warrior must be willing to fight to the death, if necessary, when his teammates need his help; and in turn each member of the team has to be able to know without any uncertainty that his teammates will do the same for him. It is this unspoken trust that defines the character of special operators. Moreover, it also means that the members of SOF units, operating alone and without the benefit of daily guidance from higher headquarters, can be trusted by their leaders, military and civilian, to act with integrity and make sound decisions that align with the best interests of the United States.

It should not surprise you that many otherwise qualified candidates are rejected each year by the recruiting teams serving SOF units. The reasons why many of these men are denied the chance to attempt selection is often attributed to something in their personal record that shows a lack of character. If you speak with any military recruiter, he or she will tell you that many young people are disqualified from entering the service because they have a history of trouble with the law or other form of authority. Their records show problems with alcohol, drugs, traffic violations and various kinds of criminal offenses such as theft, writing bad checks, domestic violence, assault, etc. Every branch of the Armed Forces has learned through decades of experience that individuals with personality or behavior issues resulting in frequent encounters with law enforcement agencies typically have difficulty adapting to military service. Likewise, an individual with a history of quitting, be it leaving high school before graduating, quitting sports teams or continuously jumping from one job to another, are all indicators that a person is probably not suited for military life, and even less so for SOF units.

Not surprisingly, an ever-increasing number of college coaches are openly stating that the deciding factor in athletic scholarship awards is a student's character as evidenced by his or her behavior during competitions, in the classroom or in other settings. If you were forced to focus on only one thing mentioned in this book, my recommendation would be to focus on the development of your character. This will have the largest impact on what you do or do not achieve; not only as an athlete, but also throughout the rest of your life!

Developing Character

As you read this chapter, this may be the first time some of you realize that SOF units aren't simply looking for physically and mentally strong men to join their ranks; but that a greater emphasis is placed on a man's character in order to decide whether or not he will be allowed into a specific unit. Unfortunately, the concepts of personal character and accountability for one's actions are not widely promoted or taught in today's public school systems, nor are they viewed with the same level of importance in American society as they once were. One only has to look at how common it is to see professional or college athletes being arrested for serious crimes or being dismissed from their teams for failure to follow team rules and other behavior that indicates various aspects of poor character.

The good news is that it is actually easy for a young person to become focused on developing their character. Hopefully, your parents have taught you the basics, such as a person should not lie, cheat, steal or otherwise behave in a manner that reflects poor character. I'm also assuming that your coaches and other adults in your life have reinforced what your parents have taught you. To enhance what you already know about this topic, we will discuss some other things that you can do regarding the development of the type or character that is prevalent in members of special operations units, champion athletes and high-achievers from all walks of life.

The Basics

As mentioned previously, at the core of personal character is the concept that a person will not lie, cheat or steal. Reflect a bit on how this applies to you and how you've lived your life so far. If you're honest with yourself, you may realize that you've fallen short on one or more occasions throughout your life. If so, you can decide that what's in the past cannot be changed, but you can make a promise to yourself that from this point forward, you will act with integrity in all that you do or say. Human beings are not perfect, and if you've made some mistakes regarding character, don't get too down on yourself – simply start becoming the person you want to be and that your current and future teammates need you to be!

Listed below are what many feel are the major traits that make up a person's character, with added detail and emphasis on how these traits apply to members of the special operations community. I think it will be rather easy for you to see how each of these traits could be applied to your own life and how they would have a beneficial impact on your overall performance as an athlete.

Integrity: The dictionary defines this quality as, *"uncompromising adherence to moral and ethical principles; soundness of moral character; honesty."*

In the SOF world, a man's word is his bond; it means that when he says something, his teammates know he's being truthful and that if he says he's going to do something, he can be counted on to do it. Of all of the traits and characteristics associated with being a successful special operator, integrity is, in my opinion, the most important of all. Having impeccable integrity at the core of one's being is the bedrock upon which all other attributes and capabilities are built.

Dependability: This quality is described as being *"a person who can be relied upon."* Dependability means that you can be relied upon by your teammates. It means that you can be counted on to do whatever is necessary, and in the SOF world, even if it means exposing yourself to dangerous conditions. This trait plays a huge role in the level of trust an operator will receive from his teammates and, along with integrity, being known as a dependable person is a critical element of serving as a member of a SOF unit.

Self-Discipline: One of the most important traits a special operator can possess is self-discipline. This trait is what enables a person to motivate and dedicate himself to a task or set of tasks that will ultimately lead to accomplishing a desired goal or objective. It is easy to follow someone's directions and perform tasks that are assigned to you. It is, however, much more difficult to take it upon yourself to perform these tasks on your own.

If you have been an athlete for more than a few years, you know that in order to improve your skills to a high level you need to do more than just show up for daily practices; you know that you will need to work on these skills (or other aspects of your training and conditioning) on your own time. You probably already know that those performing at the highest levels in your sport demonstrate high-levels of self-discipline. The same is true with the vast majority of special operators, and I dare say, the most successful people in practically every profession or vocation!

Mental Toughness: Although this quality has always been difficult to define, it is quite possibly the most important one a person must possess in order to successfully complete any of the SOF selection courses. If you ever get the chance to speak with a member of a SOF unit, I assure you that they will agree that the presence or absence of mental toughness is the major factor in determining whether or not a man successfully completes the selection process. There are various elements that comprise mental toughness that are all essential for success as a special operator and a champion athlete alike. This topic will be covered in greater detail in the Mental Toughness chapter.

Decisiveness: Special operators are constantly put in situations that will require them to assess a situation and make rapid decisions on the course of action that needs to be taken in order to achieve the desired results.

Often, these decisions must be made in the heat of battle, not unlike what you may experience in your particular sport, but of course, with much more at stake for the special operators! The development of this trait is something to which you should devote a great amount of effort. The very fact that you are reading this book and are seeking to learn from more experienced individuals is in itself an example of being decisive. Your goal, when it comes to being decisive, is to be able to make rapid and appropriate decisions under stressful situations. When participating in any sport, you will need to, very quickly, assess a situation and decide what needs to be done in order to best position yourself or your teammates for success. Decisiveness is a learned skill that special operators and athletes alike develop through experience and with the help of their mentors and coaches.

Courage: In its simplest form, courage is the ability to take action in situations that are stressful and in many cases, cause one to experience fear. To many people it may seem as though special operators do not experience fear, but they most certainly do, both in training and during actual combat operations. Through training and study, these warriors have learned how one's mind and body reacts to fear. Their understanding of the science and chemistry behind fear enables them to control it while performing their duties in highly stressful situations.

Keep in mind that courage can be displayed even when there is no threat of bodily harm. There is obviously the kind of courage that special operators need when facing necessary physically threatening situations; but there is also a form of courage that is often necessary for them to be able to do the right thing or to stand up for what they believe in. The former is called physical courage; the latter, moral courage. An example of moral courage is when you would decide to help, and in some instances, defend someone who is being bullied by older teammates, or maybe approaching a teammate who may be violating team rules or otherwise behaving in a manner that is harmful to the team. If you desire to maximize your potential as an athlete and an individual, you'll need to possess ample quantities of both forms of courage.

Resilience: Basically, *"Never give up!"* This trait is essential for special operators. Every special operations unit has a rigorous selection course that ensures that candidates' ability to hang tough and persevere despite hardship or difficulty is continuously evaluated. Quitting or sulking over setbacks, obstacles and even the serious injury or death of one or more of their teammates is not an option for special operators, for obvious reasons. These men also know that while they may begin an operation with a sound plan of attack, it is almost certain that once the first shot is fired something will happen that will render part of the initial plan unworkable. They don't stop and whine about the fact that things aren't going as they were supposed to, they simply adapt to the situation and find a way to accomplish the mission. As in the world of special operations, every sport is associated with pressure, rapidly changing situations and the need for individuals and teams to be able to adapt and perform well during times when things aren't necessarily going as planned. As an athlete, when you find yourself facing some type of obstacle, it is important to be able to figure out a way to overcome it and win.

A Navy SEAL's Thoughts on Character

Eric Greitens, a former Navy SEAL officer, in an article published in the Wall Street Journal titled *The SEAL Sensibility*, shared some of his thoughts on the infamous BUD/S training and selection course which saw only 21 of the 220 men, who had initially begun the course, standing tall on graduation day.

He spoke of a training evolution that is appropriately named *"Hell Week,"* which consists of several days and nights of virtually non-stop (the students typically get only 2-5 hours of sleep during this entire evolution) physical training and other activities, intentionally designed to produce extreme levels of physical and emotional fatigue and stress unlike anything that the students have ever typically experienced.

Greitens shared that:

> *"When the instructors really wanted to torture us, they'd say, 'Anybody who quits right now gets hot coffee and doughnuts. Come on, who wants a doughnut? Who wants a little coffee?'"*

These comments were being said to the students while they were treading water in the frigid Pacific Ocean, which is so cold, it literally causes a man's teeth to chatter after prolonged exposure to the water; and SEAL trainees get plenty of this prolonged exposure!

Greitens said:

> *"Out of the corner of my eye, I saw men running for the bell. First two men ran, then two more, and then another. The instructors had carried the bell out with us to the beach. To quit, you rang the bell three times. I could hear it: Ding, ding, ding. Ding, ding, ding. Ding, ding, ding."*

When asked to share his thoughts on what characteristics and traits are possessed by the men that succeed during this incredibly rigorous training event versus those that failed, he said:

> *"What kind of a man makes it through Hell Week? That's hard to say. But I do know-generally- who won't make it. There are a dozen types that fail: the weight-lifting meatheads; the kids covered in tattoos announcing to the world how tough they are; the preening leaders who don't want to get their hands dirty; and the look-at-me former athletes who have always been told they are stars but have never been pushed beyond the envelope of their talent to the core of their character."*

He went on to say that many of the men that made it through Hell Week were not among the strongest, fastest or most athletically gifted men in the class. Many of them were the students who *"puked on runs"* and had *"trouble with pull-ups;"* men whose *"teeth clattered just looking at the ocean;"* men who were *"visibly afraid, sometimes to the point of shaking."*

When pressed to state what he thought was a single quality that was shared by the men that succeeded during Hell Week and for that matter, BUD/S training overall, Greitens said:

> *"Even in great pain, faced with the test of their lives, they had the ability to step outside their own pain, put aside their own fear and ask: How can I help the guy next to me? They had more than the 'fist' of courage and physical strength. They also had a heart large enough to think about others, to dedicate themselves to a higher purpose."*

There are some lessons that you should recognize in Greitens' comments and reflect on relative to your own goals as an athlete. The first is that the character traits you will need to rise to the highest levels of your sport must be developed well before the most important competitions you will engage in. This character development should begin as early as possible during a young athlete's life and it should be as much of a priority as the development of his or her strength, endurance and technical skills. If you haven't done this, obviously you cannot start over, but you can start immediately to focus on enhancing and developing your character.

Unlike physical strength and endurance, and many technical skills which take many hundreds or even thousands of repetitions to perfect, character development can proceed much more rapidly. All it takes is for a young athlete to simply become aware of the concept of personal character, what traits and philosophies are associated with it; once aware, all that is needed is the desire to focus on improving and refining this critical element.

The second lesson is that you should recognize that athletic talent and sport-specific technical prowess is often useless if it is not backed up by character, or what your coaches may refer to as *"a champion's heart."* An athlete that lacks character will often fold mentally just as things are getting tough; you've probably witnessed this on one or more occasions. Even inexperienced athletes can easily recognize when one of their teammates or competitors is mentally breaking. Mental weakness is not going to enable an athlete to achieve his or her goals; and I encourage you to reflect on what you can do to steel your bodies and minds to reject any thought of quitting when things get tough during training and actual competition.

The third lesson you should take from Greitens' comments is that winners come in all shapes and sizes, and their natural talent and physical attributes vary greatly, with some of them possessing all or many of what are considered the ideal physical and athletic attributes relative to a specific sport, while others are apparently not blessed with many or even any of these same attributes, yet they win seemingly by sheer force of will and a *"refuse to lose"* mindset.

I do want to make you aware of the fact that Greitens is also an accomplished author. He's written two books that I think can be of great value to young men and women seeking self-improvement and the development of character. The first book is titled, *The Heart and the Fist: The Education of a Humanitarian, The Making of a Navy SEAL*; and the second one, *The Warrior's Heart: Becoming a Man of Compassion and Courage*. I've read them both and urge you to consider doing the same.

As you can see, character is an aggregate of qualities and traits that defines the type of person that you are, on and off the playing field. In order to be an asset to your team and to become a high level athlete, it is imperative that you focus a great deal of effort and attention to developing your character. Just as it isn't enough for a special operator to be only physically strong, it isn't enough for an athlete to be only superior in skills and conditioning to become a true champion. It requires a combination of all the attributes listed above. Character development must be at the top of your priority list if you are truly striving to maximize your potential as an athlete!

Nutrition

Previous chapters have made you aware that the members of SOF units must possess exceptional levels of physical and mental strength and endurance. It is beyond debate that the physical demands imposed by special operations training and real-world missions are incomparable to those of conventional military units. The members of SOF units are highly regarded for their actual physical prowess and athletic ability, but even more so for their sheer ability to push themselves well beyond what are considered normal boundaries of human endurance during high-stress situations.

One highly-controllable factor that has been proven to contribute to a man's successfully passing a selection course and serving as an effective member of a SOF unit is the presence of sound dietary habits that satisfy the nutritional requirements of a high-performance body. As such, the SOF community as a whole has been paying much more attention to the nutritional aspect of their training programs. A Navy SEAL officer had this to say when asked about the importance of proper nutrition to special operators:

> *"A SOF warrior needs the right nutrition and quantity of food in the same way a high performance car needs the right mixture of high octane fuel and air to achieve peak performance."*

Another special operations commander made these comments regarding the importance of nutrition relative to the health and longevity of special operators:

> *"The SOF operator is the primary weapons platform. There is an imperative to extend the operational life and maximize the battlefield performance of the operator. Nutrition is a critical component in human performance strategies."*

The comments made by these experienced special operations leaders should be studied by athletes desiring to maximize their body's strength and endurance. Typically, coaches and athletes place the most emphasis on the physical aspects of training programs – the actual exercises and physical movements that are designed to challenge the body's muscular strength and endurance levels, but often ignore the nutritional aspect. This is not a wise thing to do, because countless studies have shown that the nutritional component of an athlete's training program is as important as any other aspect of the program. The presence or absence of proper nutrition can be the difference in an athlete achieving his or her goals or failing to achieve them.

Before we continue, I do want to make it clear that not all special operators have a highly disciplined approach to their diet. Some, in fact, have dietary habits that are contrary to everything you're about to read in this chapter. I will say that most of the individuals that I am referring to were then all very young and quite physically gifted. In other words, these guys had youth on their side and were fortunate to have been born with exceptional physical capacity and abilities. They were able to perform at a high-level of physical strength and endurance while eating all types of *"junk food"* and in some instances, violating most, if not all of the other recommended guidelines regarding the use of alcohol, tobacco products, getting adequate rest, etc.

The longer you are involved in athletics, the more of these individuals you will come across. I urge you to quickly realize that, although there will always be a few individuals in any sport or profession that *seem* able to be highly successful despite *breaking the rules* associated with training and preparation. Most men and women, especially athletes, will need to exhibit discipline and follow established and proven methods in order to achieve their goals.

This chapter is focused on introducing you to some basic concepts and elements of nutrition. It will also provide an overview of several important topics related to fueling and nourishing your body as you execute your own sport-specific training program. That said, this chapter doesn't go into exhaustive detail on all aspects of nutrition, because to do so would require the entire book to be devoted to this topic! I'm writing this chapter, like all chapters in this book, assuming that those reading it are young and in the early stages of their athletic career. I'm also assuming that they have not received extensive education and training on most of the topics discussed in the book. In some instances, such as this chapter, I am trying to provide a basic level of information that will cause the reader to do additional study to gain a deeper appreciation of a specific topic. I strongly urge you to learn as much as possible about nutrition, with an emphasis on what is commonly referred to as *sports-nutrition*!

The Special Operations Nutrition Guide

I felt it would be appropriate to introduce you to a free publication titled *The Special Operations Forces Nutrition Guide*. This guide is intended to be a resource for all special operators; and it contains short summaries as well as detailed information, with worksheets, links, and important tips on various aspects of nutrition. It is exceptionally well-written and I consider it to be a credible resource regarding the topic of nutrition as related to special operators. It was produced by medical professionals and scholars with varying degrees of experience in the SOF community; and, as you will notice while reading it, everything in it is focused on the health, fitness and operational capabilities of SOF personnel.

I know for a fact that many aspiring special operators use this publication during their preparation for selection, and I think it can be of great value to young athletes that are trying to increase their level of knowledge of nutrition. Remember, the main purpose of this book is to enable the reader to gain an edge as an athlete by leveraging lessons learned by the members of SOF units and this free publication is chock-full of this type of information!

This guide can be found online on a number of SOF-related websites, simply by searching for *The Special Operations Forces Nutrition Guide* on Google or any other search engine. There are various editions of this guide, so be sure you're downloading and reading the most recent edition! When you search for this publication, you'll see a number of interesting SOF-related websites and blogs in the search results. I think you'll find some of them quite interesting!

The Basics

The human body requires fuel to function, and a steady diet of quality food, consumed at the appropriate times, enables the body to function at a high-level of efficiency for sustained periods of time. Conversely, a diet of low-quality food (lacking in nutrients), consumed at the wrong times, will eventually cause the body to break down and physical performance will deteriorate. In other words, if you provide your body with the right types of food, your physical performance will almost always improve. If you don't feed your body right, as you engage in rigorous physical activity, your body will become weaker over time, and you will face an increased risk of injury.

You've probably already heard about the benefits of healthy eating. But, as a young person trying to juggle the demands of school, sports and extra-curricular activities, you may find it difficult to stick to a healthy diet. As a result, you may have become used to eating significant quantities of *fast food* (McDonalds, Taco Bell, etc.) or worse, various types of what is commonly referred to as *"junk food."* What you may not realize is that by eating this way you are depriving your body of many essential nutrients and missing out on a number of important health benefits. This type of diet is obviously not the best way to feed your body while you undergo the rigorous physical activity that is required to achieve excellence in your sport.

Food Gives You Energy

One of the main reasons for adopting a healthy diet is because it is the fuel that your body requires in order to run. Healthy foods are typically filled with slow-digesting good carbohydrates. These foods take longer to digest than unhealthy, rapidly digesting carbohydrates so the energy they provide is released into your blood at a much slower and more stable rate. This means that you have more consistent energy levels which last for a full day of rigorous activity. In contrast, unhealthy foods generally contain high levels of bad carbohydrates. These get digested very quickly and the energy they provide is released into your blood stream all at once causing your energy levels to peak and then crash very quickly. An even worse scenario is the food that your body simply cannot digest properly.

This is what will often cause your body to have to struggle to produce various types of enzymes or other chemicals that in turn have an adverse effect in your body.

Healthy Food Ensures That Your Body Works Properly

Healthy foods are packed full of the nutrients that your body needs to operate properly. They support almost every function your body performs. For example, vitamin A is essential for healthy vision, chloride helps keep the fluid levels within your body balanced and potassium helps keep your blood pressure under control. Eating unhealthy foods deprives your body of these and many other nutrients and instead causes various reactions in your body, such as inflammation, which prevents it from functioning properly.

Healthy Food Strengthens Your Immune System

Eating a good diet can keep you safe from almost any chronic disease. Though it is still not known exactly why the nutrients in some healthy foods can protect against disease, study after study has consistently shown the power of a healthy diet when it comes to disease prevention. Another key benefit of following a healthy diet is that the wide range of vitamins, minerals and phytonutrients in these foods help keep your immune system strong. Your immune system is what keeps you safe from disease, infection and illness-causing bacteria. If you have a strong immune system then your chances of getting ill are much lower. An unhealthy diet will preclude you from supplying your body with the proper amount of nutrients, and as a result, your immune system becomes weak and your body becomes much less effective at fighting disease and infection. As an athlete, this is especially important during the later stages of the season, during which one's body is often suffering from nagging injuries, fatigue and stress. Obviously, it is important that an athlete is able to maintain an adequate level of health throughout the entire season, and healthy eating is one way to help ensure this happens.

Eating Healthy Will Improve Your Physical Performance

Eating the right foods doesn't just benefit you internally - it also greatly improves your physical performance. For example, the protein in healthy foods ensures that your muscles have the ability to repair themselves after exercise and grow back stronger. The vitamins and minerals provided by a healthy diet keep your blood healthy and ensure that it can quickly transport oxygen to where it is needed when you exert yourself.

Because much of the *fast food* that is readily available to us is lacking in the proper nutrients, it won't give you the steady release of energy that is required to complete a gruelling workout. Failing to get enough protein will prevent your muscles from fully recovering after a workout.

If you are truly serious about achieving your athletic goals, consider making a few changes to your diet! Contrary to what you may believe, eating a well-balanced diet doesn't have to be difficult or time consuming. Grabbing a piece of fruit instead of a bar of chocolate, drinking a glass of water instead of a glass of soda or cooking up some chicken and vegetables instead of having a microwave meal are all quick and easy ways to get the right nutrients into your body on a regular basis. Making smart choices such as these will do you a lot of good as you push your body through difficult training sessions.

Dietary Supplements

The members of SOF units are typically very focused on physical fitness, and they are always looking for a way of gaining an edge when it comes to enhanced strength and endurance. This often causes some of them to experiment with various types of legal, but in many cases, scientifically unproven dietary supplements. Many of these supplements have proven to be quite dangerous to certain aspects of your health, and in some instances, they have a very bad effect on individuals.

A senior enlisted leader within a Marine Corps Force Reconnaissance unit told me of an incident that occurred several years ago when his unit was participating in a training exercise in the jungles of a Central American nation. He said that the temperatures and humidity were both quite high and much higher than what was typically experienced back at the units' home base. On the second day of the exercise, several of his Marines became ill and unable to continue the long-range patrol they were conducting. The exercise had to be stopped and medevac helicopters had to be brought in to take the sick Marines to a medical facility many miles away.

This veteran Force Recon Marine was puzzled by this situation, especially since the Marines that had become ill were among the youngest and most physically fit in the unit. Initially, it was felt that these Marines had been the victims of heat exhaustion that was brought on by the high heat and humidity. Further investigation found that all of the affected Marines had been using a creatine-based dietary supplement for several weeks prior to the training exercise. When this was discovered, the doctors treating them were quickly able to verify that their symptoms (severe muscle cramps, nausea, elevated heart rates and blood pressure and varying levels of mental disorientation) matched those exhibited by other individuals that had previously experience negative reactions to the use of creatine supplements. All of the Marines recovered after several days of rest and intravenous fluids.

At that time, the use of creatine supplements was a popular fad among various types of athletes and fitness enthusiasts. Not much was known about the potential negative side-effects of this substance, but over time, it became a commonly accepted fact that it was something that should be avoided, especially by anyone that was going to exert himself for prolonged periods of time in high heat and humidity. This particular Marine Corps unit and many others in the special operations community eventually enacted a ban on the use of creatine and other unregulated and potentially dangerous dietary supplements. The reason for this prohibition is that there have been many incidents in which the use of certain dietary supplements has resulted in individuals damaging their health, and in some cases, such as the example cited earlier, becoming a liability to the teammates during training and combat missions.

Ultimately, you have to decide if you are going to use such substances, but I strongly urge you to consider avoiding them completely! It has been proven over time that a balanced diet consisting of natural foods (not processed) can provide your body with everything it needs while you engage in very demanding physical activity.

I am not saying *never* regarding the use of dietary supplements, instead, I am saying *not now*. At this point in your life and level of physical development, you can derive all of the nutrients your body needs simply through a diet of natural foods. The one exception to this is the use of a multi-vitamin after consulting with your family doctor. It is always important to consult with your personal physician, because he or she knows your complete medical history and can advise you on possible negative reactions that could result from you consuming certain vitamins, supplements, etc.

Energy Drinks and Stimulants

Energy drinks are beverages like Red Bull, Rock Star, 5-Hour Energy and Monster. I want to state right from the start that I am 100% against their use by young athletes (and anyone for that matter!). I think they are a waste of money and they are being increasingly implicated in causing serious health issues (including death) in some people. Do a Google search for *"energy drinks death"* and you'll quickly see why I don't think they are something that any serious athlete should consume.

These drinks almost always contain large doses of caffeine and other stimulants like guarana and ginseng. The amount of caffeine in an energy drink can range from 75 milligrams to over 300 milligrams per serving. To provide perspective, there are 34 milligrams in a 12 ounce can of Coke and 55 milligrams in a similar sized serving of Mountain Dew. Often, these drinks advertise that they are *"sugar-free"* and thus, do not produce what's known as a sugar-high that is typically accompanied by a sugar-crash. This simply means that these drinks contain various types of artificial sweeteners, which in their own right can cause more harm than good and are being increasingly associated with causing serious health problems.

Individual responses to caffeine vary, and some people are quite sensitive to it. The stimulants found in many energy drinks can boost the heart rate and blood pressure, dehydrate the body, and, like other stimulants, cause you to have the *"jitters"* as well as insomnia. Energy drinks pose additional risks to people who are exercising, as the combination of fluid loss from sweating and the diuretic quality of the caffeine can leave someone severely dehydrated.

Some of the claims made by the manufacturers of energy drinks such as *"improved performance and concentration"* can be misleading. These drinks are marketed as dietary supplements, and as such, current regulations do not require the Food and Drug Administration to review and approve these products before they are sold. To make matters worse, some of these drinks are produced overseas, where quality control and sanitation standards are often very poor.

In general, I recommend that you do not become addicted to caffeine in any form, be it coffee, tea or energy drinks. I certainly am advising you to never, ever put one of these energy drinks into your body!

Alcohol

By now, you are aware of the fact that you are going to have to train at a high-level in order to achieve your athletic goals. Consuming alcoholic beverages is one of the most destructive things you can do; it can literally erase or reduce the beneficial effects of your training. If you consume alcohol, you are essentially reducing your ability to develop a finely-tuned high-performing body. Seen below are some of the major reasons you should avoid consuming alcoholic beverages during your training

- Obviously, there are laws associated with consuming alcoholic beverages. If you get in trouble and get an alcohol-related incident on your record, you've greatly reduced your chances of receiving an athletic or academic scholarship, which I believe is the goal of many reading this book.

- Protein synthesis is one of the functions your body performs for repair and regrowth of muscle tissue. If you drink alcohol after a rigorous workout, you will essentially negate any benefits of the hard work you just put in and will cancel out any gains achieved from the workout.

- Dehydration is one of the worst results from consuming alcohol, lasting many hours or even days after it's consumed. Dehydration results in headaches, fatigue, balance impairment and many other problems. Your performance and recovery will be greatly diminished when drinking alcohol.

- The Human Growth Hormone is an essential part of muscle regrowth and recovery. The secretion of this hormone can be inhibited by alcohol use hindering proper recovery after workouts.

- ATP is the molecule in our cells that provides energy. Your performance will be greatly diminished due to the fact that alcohol is a toxin that can disrupt normal cell function and the production of ATP.

- Because alcohol is broken down into sugar in our bodies, it can result in unwanted weight gain from the caloric intake. Sugar becomes fat which your body stores and therefore will negatively affect your athletic performance.

- Many vital vitamins and minerals that your body uses for energy metabolism and new cell regrowth such as thiamin, zinc, folic acid and vitamin B12 won't be able to be absorbed by your body due to alcohol consumption.

- Your mental capacity for learning and retaining new information will be impaired by alcohol consumption due to the effects it can have on your sleep cycle.

- There is no nutritional value to alcohol as it only provides what are called *"empty calories."*

- The effects of large amounts of alcohol being consumed can last for as long as 3 days.

- If you decide to consume large amounts of alcohol for two consecutive nights your body and brain can be negatively impacted for up to 5 days!!!

Obviously alcohol will hinder your efforts to achieve your goals and make an already difficult task much harder.

Tobacco

The use of tobacco in any form has been proven to have negative and in some instances, fatal effects on the human body. While the use of tobacco is legal, and there are some members of SOF units (as well as some high-level athletes) who do so, I think it is safe to say that most special operators, including those who use tobacco products, would advise you to simply avoid using this substance. At best, it is an expensive habit that can harm your physical performance. At worst, the use of tobacco can literally kill you.

It is a well-known fact that tobacco contains nicotine, which can have immediate and long-term effects on your heart and vascular system. Because nicotine is a stimulant it will increase your heart rate and blood pressure very rapidly. This increase will unnecessarily tax your heart and can cause dizziness and headaches. The extra stress that is placed on your heart will inevitably reduce your athletic performance.

Testosterone is a hormone necessary for the muscle growth in our bodies. Any form of tobacco (cigarettes, chewing tobacco, dip) will damage the cells responsible for the production of testosterone and hinders the body's ability to build muscle.

When you smoke, the carbon monoxide that you inhale binds to red blood cells and disrupts the delivery of oxygen to the muscle cells. This deprivation of oxygen in the muscles greatly reduces your physical capabilities after even just a single cigarette.

A study conducted at UCLA found that there is a 4% decrease in a young person's oxygen intake after smoking. The blood vessels that carry blood and oxygen for redistribution to the muscles during exercise are impaired and constricted when you smoke. The muscles, deprived of proper oxygen levels, have to resort to an inefficient metabolic process, which results in accumulation of lactic acid within the muscle cells. Other performance issues that derive from smoking include:

- Reduced performance at all levels of physical training, decreased improvement from regular training and lower levels of endurance. A study of young adults found that endurance was reduced by 7.2 percent in smokers; and that increasing the levels of intensity in exercise resulted in smokers' inability to continue to exercise.

- Smokers have higher resting heart rates and lower maximum heart rates than nonsmokers. A higher resting heart rate means that your heart has to work harder to pump blood to all parts of your body. A lower maximum heart rate means that your heart is unable to pump the necessary additional nutrient and oxygen rich blood to the muscles during strenuous exercise.

- If you start smoking during your adolescent years, your lung function will be diminished to the point of showing early signs of obstructive airway disease; as well as slowing the normal growth of lung function, especially in girls.

- Evidence shows that young men and women who smoke are more likely to suffer exercise related injuries. It was found that among men and women who undergo Army basic training, those who smoke were approximately twice as likely to incur exercise related injuries.

- It is common for smokers with fractures of the tibia or lower leg bone to require four weeks longer than nonsmokers to heal, and some are unable to heal at all.

- Although some good athletes smoke, they would be even better if they did not. People who quit smoking demonstrate improved exercise performance compared to those who continue.

All of the above makes one thing clear – the use of tobacco products should be avoided, not only during your athletic career, but throughout your entire life!

Banned Substances

You are probably aware of the existence of performance enhancing drugs and their use by athletes in various sports. The most common of these are anabolic steroids and human growth hormone, though there are many other lesser-known substances that are classified as performance enhancing drugs. For the most part, the use of these substances is prohibited by military regulations and various federal and state laws.

As you might suspect, these substances are prohibited because research, or lack of data on their effects, have proven them to be damaging to the human body. As with alcohol and tobacco, it is best that you never use any performance enhancing drug. Your health, well-being and safety of your teammates are far more important than any temporary gains you might achieve. You can read more about the dangers of performance enhancing drugs as related to the members of SOF units in a superb document titled *The Navy SEAL Physical Fitness Guide*, which can also be found online by doing a search for the documents' title.

The main goal of this chapter was to emphasize that proper nutrition, as well as avoidance of harmful substances, is critical in maximizing your athletic potential. When you provide your body with the nutrients it needs to recover from challenging training sessions, it will be able to recover and increase its strength and endurance, which will dramatically increase your chances of achieving your goals. I urge you to do some research on your own, as well as seek guidance from your parents, coaches and family physician regarding your diet and what you can do to enhance it. Making smart choices regarding nutrition will almost always provide you with and edge over your competitors, so take action now!

Physical Training

As you know by now, the members of all SOF units must possess high levels of physical strength, endurance and stamina. In addition to these common physical attributes, the variances in the mission statements of the nation's SOF units often requires a higher degree of ability or proficiency in some specific physical skills. For instance, while all SOF units require individuals to be able to swim, the Navy SEAL mission profile demands a higher level of proficiency in surface and underwater swimming from its operators than the other more land-focused SOF units.

This surfaces the first lesson I want to convey to you in this chapter, the fact that among SOF units, there is no single physical training program or regimen that is used exclusively. Instead, these units use programs and methods that are tailored to address the specific and often, unique operational demands that are placed upon their operators. This concept is also found in the world of sports, as even novice athletes know that a training program that is highly effective for volleyball players may not be effective at all for wrestlers, cross country runners or gymnasts.

In keeping with this book's purpose of providing a broad body of special operations related knowledge and perspective that can be used by young athletes, this chapter will not offer insights on the physical training that is conducted in every SOF unit. Rather, it will provide a general overview of basic physical training concepts and principles that you should consider integrating, where and when appropriate, into your own sport-specific training program.

Like other chapters in this book, this specific chapter is being written based on the assumption that the young men and women reading it probably have not received any formal education on this topic. Thus, I am including material that I consider to be the fundamentals associated with the topic of physical training. More advanced and sport-specific information can be found in other books, various forms of media and of course, from your coaches, trainers and mentors.

The Warrior Athlete

For many years, the various branches of the military, including SOF units, conducted physical training programs that were less than effective relative to the actual functional demands of serving in combat operations. At some point, the leadership of various SOF units realized that their organizations were experiencing attrition due to injuries that might be prevented by using better designed training programs. They also began to focus these programs more toward *functional fitness*, specifically, the ability of unit members to effectively perform physical tasks on a sustained basis while in combat operations.

One example of such a program is the *Ranger Athlete Warrior* (RAW) program, which the 75th Ranger Regiment has developed and refined over the past several years. This program is one of the most scientific and comprehensive approaches to physical conditioning ever undertaken by a SOF unit. Fundamental to this program, is its holistic approach to optimizing physical performance by incorporating sound nutrition, mental preparation, and the prevention and care of injuries.

A medical officer that assisted in the creation of the program said:

> *"This holistic approach addresses every need for optimal Ranger performance. Physical training programs must be appropriate to the physical requirements, fueled by sound nutritional practices and designed to prevent avoidable overtraining and 'overuse' injuries. This program does this and also emphasizes the need for injuries, however slight, to be addressed promptly in order to prevent them from becoming more serious."*

Another medical officer associated with the ongoing maintenance and implementation of the RAW program said:

> *"The program is constantly evolving to reflect the current mindset, operations and conditions. It's an ongoing process to*

make sure we're delivering the most optimal, up-to-date program for our Rangers. Chronic issues such as back, shoulder and knee ailments affecting veteran Rangers might have been averted if today's training techniques, methodology and approach to PT had been applied in past decades."

You can read more about the *Ranger Athlete Warrior* program from various sources that can be found on the internet, including some of the actual test results and other data from the studies that were conducted when it was first being developed and implemented.

The shift in focus of physical training has led to the creation of terms such as *tactical athlete, combat athlete, warrior athlete,* and other similar terms. What you should realize is that these warrior athletes - the operators within SOF units - face a near-certainty of participating in combat operations. Adding to this burden is the fact that they must be prepared to operate in various environments known for their challenging climates and terrain. It is therefore absolutely necessary for them to constantly maintain a heightened state of physical fitness.

You should understand that in many respects, the individuals in these units have something in common with professional athletes, in the context that their bodies are one of their most important assets; and must be trained and maintained using the best knowledge and equipment available. You should view yourself in the same manner that special operators and professional athletes do regarding how they maintain their bodies and focus on maximizing their physical readiness. The sooner you adopt this mentality, the better!

Functional Fitness

As mentioned previously, special operations units have become more focused on physical training programs that create and maintain functional fitness. It is common for young athletes, especially males, to fall victim to peer pressure and the *"How much do you bench?"* type of mentality toward their physical training. Please note that during the application process for any SOF selection course, candidates will almost never be asked a question about how much weight they can press, curl or deadlift. However, they are evaluated for their ability to perform various bodyweight exercises such as pushups, pull-ups or chin-ups and sit-ups; and they definitely are evaluated relative to their ability to run and swim at certain levels of speed and endurance.

This aligns with the fact that the leadership within SOF units basically does not care how much a man can bench press, but they absolutely care about his ability to climb a rope or caving ladder, travel long distances on foot while carrying a heavy rucksack and other equipment, and other physical tasks commonly associated with the type of missions assigned to these units. The lesson here is that as an athlete, your main emphasis should be on your level of *functional fitness* relative to the actual demands of your sport.

Physical Appearance

Most people never get the chance to meet an operator from a SOF unit. This, combined with the various stereotypes about the physical appearance of operators that are promoted via Hollywood movies and the media, leads to the assumption that men serving in such units are all muscular *"physical specimens"* with six-pack abs. Although this is so in some cases, it isn't at all true of all operators. Likewise, there are many champion athletes that are of average appearance from a physique perspective. They may not look like bodybuilders or fitness models, but they manage to win, and ultimately, that's what matters most! Unless you are actually engaged in the sport of bodybuilding, you should focus less on how you look and more on how you actually perform during competition!

Principles of Exercise

Fitness professionals operate from a common understanding of several universally accepted scientifically-based principles related to physical training. When developing or refining your own specific strength and conditioning program, make sure it adheres to the following principles:

Specificity: When developing a training program it is important to first and foremost define what the major objective is. Yes, you are exercising in order to get fit; but *"Fit for what?"* For special operators, the answer is simple: *"Fit for current and potential training and combat missions."* This doesn't mean that every workout they do must look like a combat mission, but it should be a part of a larger, well-designed program. Like special operators, you should always be aware of your sport-specific goals and objectives and understand how each daily workout, done over consecutive weeks and months will help you achieve them.

Precision: Researchers have found through observation and research that some movement patterns are efficient and effective, while others are inefficient and possibly detrimental (over time, likely to lead to injury). For example, spinal, more commonly known as core, stability not only protects the spine but also creates a stable base of support from which the arms and legs can generate power. Exercises that strengthen your core are a must in order to optimize any exercise regimen and achieve optimal results from your training plan. There will be times during training when you must push yourself through fatigue and perhaps sacrifice perfect form. However, these should be the exceptions and not the everyday norms.

Balance: It is important to have a balanced approach to your training. Your program must consistently incorporate training that develops strength, endurance, and movement skills (power, agility, coordination, etc.). Taking this notion a step further, strength must be balanced by performing some workouts with body-weight resistance, some with moderate-heavy resistance, and some with a moderate resistance but higher speed (power training). Endurance should be balanced by performing a mix of aerobic and anaerobic training.

Progression: When planning your workout program it is very important to take a systematic and gradual approach to increasing the physical demands over time. For example, if you would like to increase your distance runs from 5 miles to 10 miles, you need a progression-based plan for doing so. The general rule-of-thumb is to progress time/distance by no more than 10% per week. When you do the math, you see that it will take about six weeks to safely progress from 5 miles to 10 miles. The principle of gradual progression is just as important for resistance training. Start by mastering core stability and control of body-weight exercises. Add external resistance and/or volume (number of reps over a given period of time) gradually as long as control of the movement is well-maintained. Many injuries can be traced to attempting workouts that are beyond an individual's current capability. This is quite common among younger athletes and you should ensure that you do not make this mistake.

Regularity: Obviously if you are working toward achieving optimal physical fitness, you must work out regularly and consistently. Even though that almost goes without saying, there are a couple of things to remember and keep in mind: First, if for whatever reason you cannot train for two or more consecutive weeks, assume you've lost some degree of fitness. You should then resume training at a lower level and gradually build back up. Second, even though you may be training on a regular basis, if you stop doing a particular component of your program (agility or plyometric training, for example), then you should re-master the basics of those drills before jumping back into an aggressive workout.

Variety: It has been found through a number of research studies that athletes maximize their potential by continually introducing a new focus to their exercises in an attempt to constantly force their bodies to adapt. As an example you may do a strength development program where you begin focusing on mass producing work-outs; then change the focus to power training exercises; and then finally focus on an activity-specific strength/power routine. If you always utilize the same routine, your body becomes accustomed to it and development stops otherwise referred to as *plateauing*. Maintaining variety in a program also helps to control overuse injuries. If all of your endurance training comes from running, you are more susceptible to stress-related injuries (stress fractures, tendinitis, etc.).

Overload: Just as you can plateau from lack of variety in your exercise routines; you can plateau if you do not incorporate the principle of progression into your program. However overload is when you force yourself to reach just beyond your comfort zone and run a little faster and a little farther, lift more weight or do more reps, practice agility exercises that are very difficult for you, etc. This overload is the stimulus your body needs in order to continue to improve in terms of strength, speed, endurance and agility. The challenge is to do it intelligently. <u>You must apply the principles of progression and recovery together with overload.</u>

Recovery: Overload <u>must</u> be followed by adequate degrees of recovery. Some workouts demand more recovery than others. Intense sessions that aggressively train for increase in speed, power, or heavy lifting should be followed by either a day of rest or by an easy run, swim or a mat-based core training session. It is very important to understand that the level of intensity of your workouts needs to be balanced and well thought out. You must incorporate both progression and recovery into your training cycle. In other words, for each week you must have a couple of hard workouts balanced by a couple of easier or lighter workouts. Another way of saying this is that you should not be *"maxing out"* every day, nor should you feel burned out at the end of each week. Attempting to maintain maximal workouts for several months runs the risk of overtraining, which not only leads to muscle/bone/tendon stress injuries, but also disruption of hormonal balance. If you're smart about your training program you will attain optimal fitness levels without running the risk of physical breakdown. This will be covered in more detail in the Rest and Recovery chapter.

Extreme Conditioning Programs

Most readers have probably been exposed to one or more of the more popular high-intensity workout regimens known as *extreme conditioning programs* (ECPs). Some examples of popular ECPs are CrossFit®,

P90X®, and Insanity®. These ECPs and others can be found in gyms and fitness centers in almost every city and town in America these days, and many of them can be purchased in DVD format for use in one's home or wherever he or she exercises. These programs typically consist of very challenging workouts that are based on the execution of multiple sets of high-intensity, high-volume exercises, with minimal rest periods between sets.

These programs and others of a similar nature have become increasingly popular within the U.S. military and especially within the special operations community. Many special operators find the rapid tempo of exercise sessions and the emphasis on an individual continuously challenging his physical limits to be quite appealing and motivating. For many, the opportunity to compete, even if in an informal manner, with others that are following the same workout regimen, is something that appeals to their highly-competitive personalities. Additionally, there is a perception among special operators that these programs can help them from a functional fitness perspective more effectively than many traditional forms of physical training. Some SOF units have recently integrated one or more of these programs, whole or in part, into their formal physical training programs.

Cleary, these training programs and their associated philosophies and methodologies can provide an individual with the framework of an extremely challenging fitness program. But, they have also been found to be associated with a high rate of injuries, some minor and others that are more serious in nature, among participants and especially among relatively untrained or novice fitness enthusiasts. Some of the typical injuries include muscle strains, torn ligaments, high levels of muscular soreness, stress fractures, excessive and prolonged fatigue and even mild to severe cases of a potentially life-threatening condition called *exertional rhabdomyolysis*, during which an individual's muscle tissue can literally break down and enter the bloodstream, which in turn can cause renal failure and other potentially fatal conditions.

Many of these ECP-related injuries were causing special operators to be unable to perform their duties for various periods of time. This was problematic considering the fact that SOF units have been continuously deployed to combat zones since the 9/11 terrorist attacks and they needed every operator to be healthy, fit and capable of serving with their units in combat. Due to the fact that a large number of military men and women (not just members of SOF units) were experiencing injuries while participating in these types of programs, the Department of Defense and American College of Sports Medicine convened a joint study to investigate these programs in great detail.

Results of the Study

ECPs are typically multi-dimensional programs that leverage a variety of training methods such as extensive use of body weight exercises, progressive resistance training with traditional and non-traditional weight training equipment, high-volume explosive movements and repetitions, maximum effort sprints and flexibility training. Theoretically, the variety of methods and exercises leads to the prevention of boredom and psychological burnout and also presents the body with a continuous and ever-changing series of physical challenges that can promote enhanced and accelerated fitness gains. Many participants of these programs find them to be extremely motivating and effective, with many individuals stating they are in the best shape of their lives due to their participation in this type of training. This includes a significant number of members of the SOF community, many of whom have become enthusiastic supporters of the various ECPs they personally participate in.

Most passionate ECP enthusiasts believe that these programs are low-risk, science-based, and are capable of helping men and women of all ages and fitness levels to develop a balanced physique that possesses above average levels of functional fitness for a variety of lifestyles, professions and of course, sports.

Unfortunately, the study concluded that various aspects and training practices found within some ECPs did not align with well-established safety and efficacy principles and guidelines. The nearly continuous focus on maximum effort/maximum repetitions (often at the expense of proper form or technique) - coupled with inadequate recovery time - promoted higher levels of overuse and overtraining injuries among participants.

For many, especially those that were relatively new to physical training or had little to no experience with high-intensity training, ECPs often resulted in injuries that were serious enough to prevent them from performing their duties for extended periods of time. A different problem existed among special operators that participated in ECPs. These individuals were obviously very experienced from a physical training perspective, but their highly competitive nature often led them to exceed even their capacity for high-intensity exercise and volume in an attempt to beat previous *"personal bests"* and the results produced by their teammates that were following the same ECP.

Are ECPs Good For Young Athletes?

You might conclude from the material you have just read that ECPs are dangerous and should be completely avoided, or that I am personally opposed to their use by young athletes. Neither is the case; I think that if performed under the supervision of a coach or trainer that has experience with training young athletes, ECPs can be a very effective way to gain strength, endurance and enhanced levels of flexibility. The potentially dangerous aspects of ECPs (continuous high-intensity, high-volume reps with little rest between sets and the inadequate focus on proper form or technique) can be very problematic for young athletes, especially those that have a high threshold of pain tolerance and similar amounts of the *"pain is good – more pain is better"* type of mentality toward physical training. If you are currently using an ECP as part of your training program, take some time to reflect on whether or not you are training in an intelligent manner. If you aren't using an ECP or selected aspects of one of these programs, I urge you to consider doing so, especially during the off-season. In either situation, you should discuss this topic with your coaches, trainers, your doctor and your parents.

The concepts and principles of exercise listed in this chapter can serve as the foundation of your physical training program. If applied in an intelligent and balanced manner, they will enhance your ability to engage in challenging physical training over a sustained period of time while minimizing the risk of injury. The special operations community has gained an appreciation for the *"Training smarter is better than training harder"* philosophy and has incorporated it into their unit-specific physical training programs. I encourage you to do the same!

Hydration

The importance of keeping your body adequately hydrated cannot be overstated. In fact, depriving your body of adequate levels of hydration is incredibly dangerous. Special operators are trained to understand that dehydration can quickly lead to serious injury or death, and they take extraordinary measures to ensure they are adequately hydrated at all times. It is quite common to see special operators wearing a hydration backpack during training and combat operations.

These men have been taught to adhere to a mantra that states *"hydrate or die,"* so aside from ensuring they bring enough ammunition with them on an operation, there is a heavy emphasis on how much water they will bring with them and how they will obtain more of it should the operation be of long duration.

I want to emphasize the fact that dehydration has actually resulted in fatalities in the past. Some of those who have fallen victim to the effects of dehydration have in fact been highly-conditioned special operators and athletes. It is of the utmost importance that you heed this warning and employ responsible measures to prevent a situation in which you might suffer the same fate. Hydration is as essential as food and one of your major responsibilities as an athlete is to ensure that you are properly hydrated at all times!

You must maintain proper hydration in order to:

- Prevent fatigue and muscle cramps.

- Maintain a lower heart rate for longer periods of time (this is another reason heart rate monitors are so important).

- Hydration prevents your body from overheating and going into heat stroke. You need to sweat when you are hot; it is a cooling mechanism built-in to your body's functions. When you are properly hydrated before and during a workout you are able to sweat as much as necessary so your body can stay at its optimal temperature.

- Water acts as a lubricant for muscles and joints and it helps cushion joints to keep muscles working properly.

- Approximately 70-75% of muscle is made up of water, so maintaining the right water balance is necessary for peak muscle performance.

- Studies have shown that as little as a 1% loss in fluids can create a performance degradation of 2% in athletes.

Heat Exhaustion and Heat Stroke

It is a scientifically-proven fact that an athlete that is dehydrated will inevitably experience diminished performance during training and competition. You should be aware of the sad fact that every year several young athletes die as a result of dehydration – when the body does not have enough fluid in it - which typically leads to dangerous conditions known as *heat exhaustion* and *heat stroke.*

When the human body is exposed to high temperatures for long periods of time; or is engaged in prolonged periods of vigorous activities, two very dangerous conditions known as heat exhaustion or heat stroke can occur. These conditions are often brought on by the fact that an individual is already somewhat dehydrated prior to engaging in strenuous exercise or is taking certain medications such as antihistamines, blood pressure medication, or antidepressants.

As you know, your body sweats when it is overheated from exercise or simply by being in high temperatures. Sweating is your body's natural cooling function and simply stated, it is the way your body removes excessive heat so it is able to operate at the temperature range that it was designed for. Sweat typically evaporates from the skin, transferring the heat to the air as this happens, to help cool the body. It is harder for sweat to evaporate if:

- The humidity is high

- An individual is wearing tight or layered clothing that covers most of the skin

- An individual is dehydrated, which will cause you to produce less sweat

Heat Exhaustion

Heat exhaustion, while a less serious condition than heat stroke, is still a condition that can cause great injury to a person. It can cause damage to the body's *"cooling system"* that literally can cause an athlete to be required to stop practicing and competing for several months or even permanently. Symptoms of heat exhaustion can include:

- Normal or only slightly elevated body temperature

- Cool, moist (clammy), pale skin

- Sweating (sometimes heavily)

- Headache

- Nausea/vomiting

- Dizziness/weakness/fatigue

- Rapid pulse

- Decreased blood pressure

- Dark or tea-colored urine

- Muscle cramps

- Rapid/shallow breathing

To respond to heat exhaustion:

- Move the person into shaded area or an air conditioned space.

- Loosen clothing or remove as much clothing as possible.

- Drink cool water or non-alcoholic, non-caffeinated beverages like sports drinks to help restore electrolyte balance.

- Take a cool shower or sponge bath.

- Spray cool water on yourself and sit in front of a fan or have others fan you.

- Massage or stretch cramping muscles.

- Monitor your temperature for changes in your condition that suggest heat stroke (see below).

- Seek emergency treatment or call 911 if attempts to decrease body temperature fail or if you experience chest pain, abdominal pain, persistent vomiting so that you can't keep down fluids, or if you develop any of the symptoms of heat stroke (see below).

Heat Stroke

Heat stroke is a life-threatening situation in which the body loses its ability to cool itself, largely because it has already sweated out all of the available water in a person's body. When this happens, the person generally stops sweating and begins to overheat just like a car's engine does on a hot summer day. The difference between the two is that the car's engine will simply stop running when it overheats, but the human body will die. Heat stroke is associated with very high internal body

107

temperatures, sometimes as high or higher than 106 degrees Fahrenheit. Heat stroke can result in death if it is not treated promptly. Symptoms include:

- Very high body temperature (usually over 104 degrees F)
- No sweating
- Hot, dry, red skin
- Rapid pulse
- Difficulty breathing

If body temperatures aren't quickly reduced, heat stroke symptoms can progress to:

- Confusion, irritability, disorientation, or hallucinations
- Seizures
- Loss of consciousness and coma
- Death

If you think one of your teammates or another competitor has heat stroke, immediately inform your coaches, the athletic trainers or medical crew at the event and if you cannot find them, tell any other adult in the area and ask for assistance. Make sure that someone calls 911. While waiting for medical help, you should:

- Move the person into the shade or into air conditioning.

- Elevate their feet higher than their head to reduce the chance of shock.

- Remove clothing and attempt to cool them down by wrapping them in a cool, wet sheet or spraying them with cool water and fanning them.

- Put ice packs or cold compresses under their arms, on their groin area, and behind their neck.

- Give them cool drinks only if they are not disoriented and not vomiting.

- Stay with them until medical help arrives.

Hydration Tips

You've probably heard that the general rule is to drink 8 glasses of water per day or 64 ounces. However, studies show that an average person doing an average amount of activity every day needs to drink half of his or her weight in ounces. So if you weigh 200 pounds you must drink 100 ounces of water per day (or about 12½ 8-oz glasses of water per day).

Regardless of a person's size and athletic pursuits there are two simple measures of proper hydration levels:

If you are excreting a large amount of light colored urine (almost clear) you are most likely properly hydrated. But if your urine seems dark and concentrated (very yellow/orange colored) you need to increase your water intake because you are most likely dehydrated.

Monitor your weight before you exercise and after. Anything you've lost during your workout is probably a loss of fluids so drink enough to replace what you've lost. And if you've gained any weight during exercise you may actually be drinking more water than necessary.

The longer your workouts, the more water intake you'll need in order to maintain proper hydration levels. Inappropriate hydration will negatively affect and diminish your performance. Studies have shown that people who sweat away as little as two percent of their body weight have a drop in blood volume; and when blood volume drops their heart has to pump extra hard to circulate blood. The harder your heart has to work to pump blood, the harder your entire body is working just to maintain the level at which you are exercising – there is little room for increased performance. You can tell how hard your heart is working by using a heart rate monitor. It's important to note also that a decrease in blood volume can lead to muscle cramps, dizziness, fatigue, heat exhaustion and even heat stroke, which can be fatal.

Weigh yourself before you work out. After you've weighed yourself, hydrate by drinking 15-20 ounces of water 2 to 3 hours before exercise; then drink 8-10 ounces of fluid 30 minutes before you begin. It is equally important to hydrate during your workout. Water and electrolytes play very important roles in proper body functions during activity. Drinking 8-10 ounces of water for every 15 minutes of exercise is a good rule of thumb. After you finish exercising weigh yourself so you can replace any fluids you released during your workout. A good general guideline is 20-24 ounces of water for every pound you've dropped during your workout.

Though this chapter is brief, it addresses one of the most important topics associated with the safe training and development of athletes. I recommend that you speak with your coaches, athletic trainers and family physician regarding ways you can maintain adequate hydration while engaging in your specific sport.

Heart Rate

In a subsequent chapter, you will learn about the human body's predictable reactions to what is commonly referred to as the *human stress response*. One of these reactions is the elevation of a person's heart rate. Exercise physiologists and other medical professionals believe that increased heart rate has a highly negative impact upon an individual's performance during periods of high-stress and perceived danger. Military and law enforcement trainers have long known about the negative effects of elevated heart rate relative to the mental acuity and decision-making ability of men operating in high-risk, dangerous situations and they have addressed this issue by adapting their training programs and methods.

The special operations community has been particularly active regarding the adoption of heart-rate related knowledge. Trainers in all SOF units are continuously refining techniques designed to help special operators maintain their heart rates at levels that have been proven to facilitate critical thinking, decision-making and use of fine motor skills. This issue – elevated heart rate as a reaction to the human stress response – is one that has direct application to the world of sports. It is a topic that you should study and learn more about; and I think that integrating the monitoring and tracking of your heart-rate during various phases of your training program is one of the most important things you can do to reach your maximum potential as an athlete.

The Importance of Heart Rate

In 1995 a U.S. Army officer named Lieutenant Colonel David Grossman wrote a book titled, *On Combat: The Psychology and Physiology of Deadly Conflict in War and in Peace.* One of the topics covered in this book is the importance of heart rate relative to an individual's ability to perform certain tasks during the stressful situations typically experienced by combat soldiers, police officers and other law enforcement personnel.

His research, which has been validated by previous and subsequent studies, indicates that in general, the higher the heart rate, the more a human body relies on instincts when responding to dangerous situations, threats or unexpected problems. The problem with this is that typically, without training, during times of great stress, a person's instincts are often wrong. In a combat situation, an incorrect decision or poorly executed physical action can result in death, injury or mission failure. Though the ramifications are not as serious for athletes, the fact is that their bodies share the same genetically hard-wired response to stress and danger; and failure to control these natural reactions can seriously degrade athletic performance.

Grossman's research led to his creation of five color-coded conditions based on a person's heart rate:

White - The normal heart rate range is 60-80 this is the classification of white. At this heart rate thought processes are normal fine motor skills are intact and gross motor skills can perform daily activities.

Yellow - When fear causes the release of adrenalin the heart rate begins to climb and reaches the next level, the heart rate is 80-115 in condition yellow. Condition yellow is different from condition white because the level of vigilance increases. Condition yellow could be compared to what you would feel walking down a dark alley known for violence. If the heart rate continues to increase the individual will reach condition red.

Red - Condition red is when the heart rate is between 115 and 145. This is considered to be the optimal performance level. Condition red has the benefit of increased strength, reaction time, and speed but the individual will have a loss in fine motor skills.

Grey - A heart rate from 145-175 is called condition grey, and it's reserved for special operations units who train to work at this level. There is no difference between red and gray except for the extensive training the operator has undergone, which enables him to work in this condition for a period of time.

Black - The last condition, black, is when the heart rate is above 175. In condition black irrational behavior, paralysis, loss of bowel control, loss of urine control and loss of gross motor skills are at the maximum level. Escaping from the threat is the only thing that the person is able to do.

It is important that you realize that in many situations, elevated heart rates are less the result of physical stress than they are of psychological stress. Think of a time in your life when you were sitting down or were not moving at all, yet your heart was racing as if you'd just done several wind sprints or ran up a few flights of stairs. The two main points being presented are, the ability of the mind to cause physiological responses in one's body, and of course, the need to control these responses to the point they do not have a negative impact on performance.

It is also essential that you realize that the five conditions of heart rate established by Colonel Grossman are not to be considered *"etched in stone,"* or serve as literal boundaries that cannot be crossed. It is a fact that many highly trained people engaged in a variety of activities often operate at peak efficiency with heart rates as high as 200 bpm for extended periods of time. World class cross country skiers and Formula I race car drivers are just two examples of this.

One scientific study of seasoned and highly conditioned Army Special Forces operators indicated that men with the best results on various tests and tasks could do so at heart rates at or just below 175 bpm. However operators that experienced heart rates above 175 bpm turned in some of the worst results in the study. But, the general thought amongst military leaders and medical personnel is that a special operator can be educated and made aware of how his mind (when experiencing fear or threat stress) can affect his body, and be trained on how to counter and minimize its negative impact on performance.

In fact, all special operations units utilize a technique during various training sessions in which the heart rates of operators are purposely elevated prior to the session or a specific round of training. An example of this is during certain types of marksmanship training in which the operators are required to shoot to established standards under a variety of conditions. Prior to beginning their graded runs through the course of fire, they are made to do several wind sprints or perform certain exercises in order to get their heart rates elevated before they begin shooting for score.

SOF trainers know that in an actual combat situation, the heart rates of the operators will likely be elevated due to physical exertion and the effects of the human stress response. Because elevated heart rates have an effect on visual acuity and fine motor skills, both of which are very important when shooting, SOF trainers know that it is highly beneficial for operators to practice shooting while their bodies and minds are experiencing stressors that are like those that will be present during combat situations. This technique is also used in the world of sports, where athletes are required to drill techniques or perform certain skills or tactics when fatigued to the same levels they'll likely experience during the late stages of a game or match.

Monitoring Your Heart Rate

Over the past twenty-five years or so, with the introduction of personal heart rate monitors that can be purchased for as little as $50, the practice of monitoring heart rate has become increasingly popular by an ever-increasing number of athletes and fitness enthusiasts as they seek to maximize their physical potential. A large percentage of special operators also use these devices when they engage in physical training. I am strongly suggesting that you purchase one of these devices and begin to monitor and track your heart rate during training sessions and rest/recovery periods.

One way you'll benefit from monitoring your heart rate is simply to track your progress. When you begin a training regimen, whether as a beginner, or as an accomplished athlete, you want to see results. A heart rate monitor (HRM) will pick up even the smallest of changes in your heart rate, thus alerting you of a possible problem even before you are aware something has changed. These changes can indicate that you are exercising with too much or too little intensity, whether your level of hydration is inadequate or in some instances, they may indicate problems with your heart or other health issues. Once you use a HRM for several weeks, you become aware of what your typical heart rate is before, during and after various training activities. Thus, you'll be able to detect any changes from your normal heart rate while training and during your rest and recovery phases.

Training without use of a HRM can often result in overtraining and, ultimately, diminished physical performance. Younger athletes, in particular, are susceptible to overtraining due to extreme quantities of high-intensity training. Continuous training at high levels of intensity is at odds with the body's need for rest and recovery. This ultimately leads to physical and mental fatigue and, of course, the probability of diminished performance during competitive events. Using a HRM is an effective way of ensuring your recovery time is appropriate for the intensity of your work outs.

Reasons to use a heart rate monitor:

- A HRM takes the guesswork out of it so you can simply focus on training properly and efficiently to achieve your fitness goals.

- It helps you ensure your recovery time is appropriate for the intensity of your work outs.

- You can more quickly figure out if other factors are affecting your health by simply tracking your Resting Heart Rate when you wake up and at other times during the day.

The most common type of heart rate monitor consists of an elastic chest strap that fastens around the chest and wirelessly transmits continuous heart rate data to a wristwatch-style receiver. Models range from basic to advanced, and the prices for them vary from approximately $50 to several hundred dollars. I recommend that you purchase and use one of the basic models, as they possess all of the capabilities you will need during your physical training program. There are also some good books available for you to better inform yourself, two examples are: *Heart Rate Training* by Roy Benson and Declan Connolly and *Total Heart Rate Training: Customize and Maximize Your Workout Using a Heart Rate Monitor* by Joe Friel.

This chapter is intended to be a general introduction to the concept of monitoring your heart rate during your athletic training. I recommend that you seek additional information on this topic from your physician, coaches, trainers and the numerous and credible online sources that are available.

Rest and Recovery

It is important that you understand that hours of practice and countless repetitions are not a guarantee of athletic success. Although a lot of hard work is required to maximize your potential as an athlete, this hard work will prove less effective if it is not combined with adequate recovery time, which in turn gives the body a chance to regenerate and adapt to the training you're doing. If done properly, recovery enables an athlete to realize the maximum benefits of a workout and feel rested and strong for the next training session or competition.

I want to emphasize that the material in this chapter is not focused on the selection and assessment courses or processes utilized by various SOF units. The physical and mental stress that selection courses subject candidates to is necessary in order to identify those that possess the required levels of mental toughness, self-discipline, resiliency, etc. Quite frankly, the instructors or evaluators actively seek to push men to the brink of their physical and mental limits and depriving them of sleep and other forms of rest helps them do so. Once assigned to an operational unit, these men will still participate in very intense physical activities, but the difference is that at this point, they've proven themselves to be worthy of serving in a SOF unit. Now, their leaders will obviously want to ensure that these men stay as healthy and strong as possible.

Several years ago, the special operations community as a whole decided to implement, where appropriate, some of the knowledge and training methods found at the highest levels of professional and amateur sports. The reason for this was simple; as a result of years of continuous and intense training, special operators were experiencing physical and psychological injuries and conditions that were rendering them temporarily or permanently incapable of performing their duties. It takes several years and millions of dollars to produce a fully-trained special operator, and sadly, SOF units were losing an unacceptable number of operators due to injuries that were largely preventable. The loss of these operators had a profoundly negative impact upon the combat readiness and effectiveness of these units, and the leadership within the special operations community began to take steps designed to reverse the steadily accelerating trend of the *"broken operator."*

During a conversation I had with a highly experienced Air Force special operator, he said:

> *"Looking back on my long experience in special operations and from my observations of operators from other SOF units, those of us who took the necessary down-time to rest and relax, more often than not were able to resume training and*

deployment cycles with a renewed sense of purpose coupled with a fresh mind and body. Considering the physical and mental stress we are consistently exposed to, I believe that we need that down-time to heal any physical injuries we may have, to address any psychological burnout or issues related to one's level of motivation and commitment to the unit, and to think about what we learned from the most recent training cycle and deployment. I think that without some kind of a break, during which an operator can mentally and physically disengage from the demands of serving in a SOF unit, the mind and body can potentially become stale and overworked to the point of it negatively affecting our performance in training and during combat operations. I also think it can diminish the satisfaction that we get and need from serving in our respective units."

I believe that everything he said about the need for rest and recovery among special operators also applies to athletes, especially those that are highly committed and might have a tendency to let their desire to *"train hard"* result in overtraining.

A long-serving NCO from the 75th Ranger Regiment had this to say about the topic of sleep:

"Anyone who knows anything about Rangers knows that we take pride in our ability to operate for long periods of time

without sleep. While this ability has obvious advantages when we are participating in dynamic and around-the-clock combat operations, it also tends to create a mindset among us, particularly among the younger Rangers, that sleep is a luxury or something that really doesn't have to be a priority for remaining combat ready.

I began to learn more about the value of adequate rest and recovery, specifically in the area of sleep, when a medical doctor joined our headquarters unit. He had done extensive research on this topic and I eventually discovered that he was considered one of the special operations community's experts in this area. Long story made short, once I started paying attention to my sleep habits and ensuring I was getting a solid 7-8 hours of sleep per night (obviously, I was not always able to do this during training or while deployed) my physical strength and endurance were both greatly improved.

I also noticed that my mind functioned better far longer into the day. Prior to getting the proper amount of sleep each night, I often felt lethargic starting around 2pm or so and after I began giving my body and mind the rest it needed, I realized that I was feeling great throughout the entire day. I think that one of the best habits a young athlete can acquire is ensuring that he or she is getting enough sleep each night; I think it would make a huge difference in their performance."

Anyone that has been around sports for any length of time probably knows of one or more athletes that insisted on training at a high level during the off season without taking a break before the regular season began. While these athletes were able to perform at a high level at the beginning of the regular season, when the most important part of the season began, the district, regional, state and national championships, they often did not perform well, and in some instances, they failed miserably.

Many of these athletes had simply peaked too soon in the season, many sustained overuse injuries or showed the effects of overtraining; and for many of them, the high degree of motivation and drive that was so apparent during the off-season and the early part of the season had almost disappeared. Experienced coaches know that it is very difficult and risky for an athlete to try to sustain a high level of physical intensity and mental focus for a long period of time without a break. The aim of this chapter is to emphasize the importance that rest and recovery plays in the prevention of overtraining and its associated physical and psychological injuries.

Overtraining

Overtraining is a physical, behavioral, and emotional condition that occurs when the volume and intensity of an individual's training exceeds their recovery capacity. An athlete that has overtrained will cease making progress and eventually will begin to lose strength, stamina and endurance. Overtraining typically leads to *overuse injuries*, which result from the stresses placed on your body when performing excessive and often, technically incorrect repetitions or movements. An athlete that is overtrained is also very susceptible to *burnout*, which is a condition in which an athlete becomes psychologically fatigued to the point that he or she lacks the desire and motivation to practice and perform at a high-level of intensity. Burnout actually causes many young athletes to drop out of their sport.

Recovery

Recovery is a common term used to describe how an individual's body adapts to the demands of a training session or competition. This ability to adapt is both physical and psychological and ideally is associated with the restoration of an individual's level of energy, strength and endurance. Inadequate recovery, whether physical or psychological, will inevitably result in diminished performance, overuse injuries and what is commonly referred to as *"burnout,"* which means an athlete no longer has the passion or desire to train and compete. The obvious goal is to prevent these conditions through adequate periods of rest and recovery.

It's not a secret that to become a high-level athlete, an individual is going to have to work very hard, pushing his or her body and mind through many years of rigorous training. If done intelligently, utilizing a balanced approach, athletes can enjoy a long and successful career. However, if an athlete fails to consider the need for the appropriate amounts of recovery, ultimately his or her body will break and along with it the desire to remain a competitive athlete.

The obvious solution is for an athlete, with his coaches, to determine the proper mix of training (sessions of varying physical intensity) and recovery that enables the attainment of excellence while also avoiding injuries. In this regard, the special operations community has adopted philosophies and methods that have proven effective in the world of high-level sports. Realizing that the continuous exposure of the human body to nearly continuous intense physical activity was resulting in the loss of many highly-trained operators, the leadership within SOF units began placing greater emphasis on the proper blend of training and recovery. As a result, the members of these units are experiencing fewer non-combat related injuries and they are retaining significant strength, flexibility and endurance much longer than in the past. As an athlete, you'd be wise to reflect upon the concept of recovery and ensure that you are paying attention to this critical aspect of your training program.

Passive and Active Rest

One of the most important things you can learn from this chapter is that athletes that insist on pushing their bodies through high-intensity workouts on a daily basis are setting themselves up for failure. Aside from the very small percentage of individuals who are blessed with an extraordinary degree of physical and mental durability, the reality is that the majority of athletes must provide their bodies with adequate rest and recovery between training sessions. This can be done using *active rest* and *passive rest*. It is critical that you understand the difference between the two and how they, when properly used, can help you achieve your goals as an athlete.

Passive rest

When we hear the term rest, most people think about sleeping or lying on the couch watching television. This form of rest is called *passive rest*. Obviously, everyone needs to get high-quality sleep each night, especially athletes engaging in intense physical training, but aside from nightly sleep, it is generally considered counterproductive for an athlete to engage in significant amounts of passive rest as a means of recovery. In other words, the degree and pace of recovery is often diminished if an athlete simply sleeps or lays dormant between training sessions, and most athletic trainers agree that an athlete should not engage in passive rest (aside from sleeping at night) more than once per week and preferably, once every 10-14 days.

Active rest

Active rest is when an athlete, after an intense training session, engages in sub-maximal exercise. An active rest workout provides your body the opportunity to promote the increased flow of blood, which is critical to the recovery process. This form of rest has been proven over time to produce better results than passive rest, assuming that the athlete ensures the active rest sessions are truly low-intensity. It is critical that athletes and coaches alike understand that <u>active rest means low intensity</u>! If active rest activities are allowed to escalate into high intensity training sessions, injury and psychological burnout are sure to follow.

Like special operators, athletes at all levels face a lot of pressure to perform well and produce results. This can lead athletes, coaches and parents to adopt a *"winning at all cost"* mentality that often leads to excessive training and lack of proper rest and recovery, which in turn typically results in physical and/or psychological injuries. Obviously, the injured athlete will not be able to perform at his or her peak level.

The information in this chapter can help you create a balanced training program that effectively meshes intense physical activity (practice and actual competition) with adequate periods of recovery and rest. Using a balanced approach to training, which incorporates a well-thought out rest and recovery strategy is typically a very poorly understood training principle among athletes and their parents and coaches. Although it is important to do the training necessary to increase strength, flexibility, endurance and sport-specific skills, it is just as important to give your body the rest it needs in order to allow the recovery period your muscles require to be able to regenerate and be fully prepared for the next training session or competition... You see, it's a cycle!

Practice

As a result of their extensive training, every member of a special operations unit acquires a deep appreciation for the value of practice – the repetitive execution of skills and techniques – as a major factor in the development of excellence. In fact, during my many conversations with special operators on this topic, all of them agreed that what they had learned about skill training and practice would have been very useful during their athletic careers. They all felt this knowledge would have had a very significant effect on their entire outlook and approach to their sport. This chapter will provide you with invaluable information and lessons learned by men who have taken the journey to excellence. What these warriors have enabled me to share with you can play a huge role in your development not only as an athlete, but in many aspects of your personal and professional life.

Champions – Born or Built?

In the past, many people held to the belief that in order to be great at something, you had to have been born with a specific talent. They believed that those who were able to reach the top were the lucky few.

This view was very prevalent in the world of sports and even today, many coaches and athletes cling to these beliefs. This theory – that to be great at something, you have to be born with *"greatness"* - has pretty much been blown out of the water. Countless studies – and history – have shown that belief to be inaccurate. If you were to conduct research just about any so-called *"high-achieving"* person in any field, what you would find is a testament to the fact that through dedication, discipline and practice you can in fact achieve excellence.

All of the above is especially true in the world of special operations. Though the recruiters for every SOF unit are guided by a detailed profile designed to help them identify individuals capable of making it through the selection process, the truth is that the majority of these *ideal candidates* fail. The seasoned special operators that I've spoken with on this topic agree that there are two major factors in determining whether or not a man passes selection and performs well in the rigorous training as a member of a SOF unit: the first is mental toughness, (or what some experienced operators refer to as *heart* or *grit)*, and the second is a man's ability to remain focused while participating in nearly continuous periods of stressful *deliberate practice.*

In other words, in the special operations community, many of the men who eventually become members of the most elite units are those who simply had the unwavering desire to do so. They ultimately achieved their goals by engaging in the focused and relentless study and self-improvement that is associated with deliberate practice.

Likewise, relative to becoming a champion athlete, I think that rather than having natural aptitude or talent, it is more important that an athlete must truly *"love"* to compete. This love or affinity for the battle – the test of one's character and skills against high-level competition - will be the biggest influence on how badly he or she wants to reach the heights of any sport. It is this competitive fire that leads to the desire to excel, which ultimately drives special operators and athletes alike to dedicate themselves toward doing whatever it takes to become an elite performer. I wish that I could tell you that what you just read is the secret formula that will magically elevate your performance as an athlete, but sadly, this is not reality. There simply isn't a quick or easy way to go about becoming a champion athlete. It will take a lot of practice, specifically, deliberate practice, to maximize your potential and reach the heights of your sport!

Quality of Practice

"Practice makes perfect" is a phrase you have probably heard many times throughout your life. But it is important to note that simply repeatedly doing something you already know how to do does not qualify as 'practice.' Rather, performing a skill or technique with precision each and every time, or, said another way, engaging in *perfect practice* is what results in superior performance in the heat of battle, for both special

operators on a battlefield in some far-away country and athletes in a gym, stadium or other venue.

Dr. Anders Ericcson, a Swedish psychologist and one of the world's most respected authorities on the topic of high performance, emphasizes the fact that not only is the quantity of practice important, but probably more important is the quality of your practice. He calls this enhanced, more focused, detailed and meticulous kind of practice *"deliberate practice."*

Deliberate practice, or *perfect practice*, is a mindset that is deeply ingrained in the students going through special operations selection and training. Interestingly, at the time that most operators were going through their respective selection courses, they often didn't realize the impact that the incessant repetition of drills was having on them from a mindset perspective. At that point, most were simply trying to survive whatever training evolution they happened to be undergoing, and hopefully, making it through another day of the selection course! It became evident to these men, at some point later on, that the purpose of the repetitive drills is not only to teach them how to do something, but to teach them how to focus on constantly improving on their skills. Their training sessions are designed in such a way that the final outcome will result in not only proficiency but in excellence. This mindset – the relentless pursuit of excellence – is something that you should reflect upon and consciously apply to your athletic training.

Deliberate Practice

Practice has been scientifically shown to have an incredible impact on a person's performance in countless skills, techniques, procedures, etc. But, for athletes, it isn't enough to simply go out and conduct the same drills day after day. *Deliberate practice* is the constant, intense and detailed practice that you conduct in order to improve on individual and specific skills. When you conduct deliberate practice you need to break down the skills you need to improve on into discrete segments. For example, if you are a cross country runner, you can break down the way you train into categories such as speed, endurance, breathing, pace and form. You can then create a training plan that consists of individual practice sessions that are tailored to focus on one or more of these categories. An example of a training plan that is focused on the concept of deliberate practice could entail:

- Speed focused workouts – For this type of workout a runner must be focused solely on speed. He or she would run a predetermined distance at the fastest sustainable pace for a specific period of time followed by a short period of rest before repeating the process.

- Endurance focused workouts - would require you to run long distances; always gradually increasing the distance.

- Breathing focused workouts - would mean that throughout your entire workout, whether speed or endurance, the only thing you are thinking about and executing is your breathing rhythm (this is harder than it sounds).

- Pace focused workouts - would mean that you would run mile intervals focusing solely on maintaining the same exact pace every single time.

- Form focused workouts - means that you would direct your attention to how high you are lifting your knees and arms, and on locking your core so that your back is perfectly supported.

Practicing all of these things separately, but in a deliberately crafted manner, will generate the muscle memory that will come together during a race. At some point in your training, you will no longer even need to think about the various components of running (those listed above) because you will have practiced them so much that they will become second nature. This concept applies to any sport-specific skills and techniques you wish to perfect.

The 10,000 Hour Rule

Dr. Ericcson conducted a scientific study that produced results showing that an average of 10,000 hours of practice is required in order to achieve *greatness* or, put another way, to become an expert at a specific skill. Now, this famous *"10,000 Hour Rule"* refers to the number of total hours of practice and study conducted by individuals that had achieved greatness in various fields such as business, sports, music, academia, the medical profession, etc. While some experts do not agree with the validity of the 10,000 hour rule, most do agree with the overall concept, which essentially asserts that achieving excellence and mastering a skill doesn't happen in a week or a month, it takes many years of hard work and dedication.

From a special operations perspective, most experienced operators that I have discussed this issue with agree that the 10,000 hour rule applies to the development of a seasoned and well-rounded special operator. In other words, while young men can be trained to a high-level of proficiency in many special operations-related skills over the course of a couple of years, the real experts, those who stand out as the premier operators within SOF units are those that typically possess ten or more years of operational experience.

It is at this point that many SOF leaders feel an operator has truly seen and done just about everything relative to executing the missions assigned to his specific unit; and possesses the *expert knowledge* that enables him to be an effective leader and mentor to less-experienced teammates. When asked specifically about the 10,000 hour benchmark relative to achieving expert status as a special operator, the men I spoke with all believed that it was applicable to their specific situation and that most highly-tenured operators had actually exceeded this benchmark. In other words, they spent years learning and perfecting their skills; and even after attaining expert status, they continued to study, practice and gain additional levels of expertise relative to special operations.

An excellent example of deliberate practice is the Close Quarter Battle (CQB) training that special operators undergo. I'll use the Navy SEALs to illustrate this concept, but you should know that all SOF units that conduct CQB training follow the same general training pattern and flow. When young sailors first begin their training to become Navy SEALs, they enter a course called BUD/S (Basic Underwater Demolition/SEAL). BUD/S is the selection course that is the gateway to the SEAL community. During the final phase of the course, the students are exposed to the basics of small arms and learn how to operate various types of individual weapons. As they acquire a basic appreciation for the fundamentals of combat shooting, they (with the help of their instructors) begin to identify their strengths and weaknesses relative to the use of small arms and focus on attaining prescribed levels of proficiency.

Once the students graduate from BUD/S, they begin an intense period of follow-on training, and it is during this training that they are subjected to an intense amount of deliberate practice designed to produce operators that meet the basic standards for CQB operations. During this training, the students will repeatedly execute various CQB-related drills that focus on skills such as shooting accuracy, reloading and clearing weapon malfunctions while moving as part of an assault team, transitioning from using their rifle to their pistol, moving with their team as they enter and clear buildings and other structures, etc. All of these elements are constantly practiced in carefully arranged and increasingly difficult scenarios.

After many hours of practice (with constant feedback and coaching from the instructors), the students, assuming they meet the standards when tested, are now considered to possess a level of proficiency that enables them to function effectively as part of an assault team in an operational SEAL unit. That said, these men are still very new to CQB operations and still have much to learn. Once they arrive at their operational unit, they will continue to practice and practice, and practice some more, until the various skills associated with CQB operations becomes instinctive, and the actions that their bodies are required to execute become deeply ingrained in their muscle-memory.

At this point, their ability to execute and perform CQB skills during high-stress situations (actual combat operations) is very much like that of high-level athletes performing during the most critical and intense periods of competition. It all goes back to the concept of deliberate practice, which focuses on the acquisition of fundamental knowledge and skills that are honed to perfection via continuous and repetitive training that is guided by the *"perfect practice makes perfect"* mentality. This is how novices are gradually made into champions!

I asked John, who had served as both an enlisted man and commissioned officer in the Army's famed 75th Ranger Regiment, for his thoughts on the concept of practice as it is done within Ranger units; and how young athletes could benefit from adopting some of the same philosophies and methods. Here are his comments:

> *"Ranger units are the 'shock troops' of the special operations community. Often, they are operating in direct support of one or more of another SOF unit and their role in the operational plan is almost always associated with stealth, speed, precision and violent actions once engaged with an enemy force. Many missions require the precise and timely application of various types of weapons and high explosives. Mistakes of any type can result in mission failure and the loss of life or serious injury among the members of the various units that are participating in any given mission."*

> *To minimize the potential for mistakes, Ranger units practice their individual and unit skills relentlessly and with a sense of purpose rarely seen outside of the special operations community. Their training programs and methods have been refined over many years of experience in peace time and during combat operations, and they have gained a true appreciation for the value of men performing various skills and techniques hundreds and in some cases, thousands of times in order to achieve the* "muscle memory" *that enables these warriors to perform with speed and precision during*

dangerous and high-stakes situations, many of which happen in total darkness.

After I had been in the Regiment for a few years, I often wondered how my performance as a high school and college athlete would have differed if at that time I had the same level of self-discipline, attention to detail and appreciation for "perfect practice" that I had gained since becoming a member of a Ranger unit. As I write this, with the benefit of many additional years of experience and perspective, there's no doubt in my mind that I would have achieved more as an athlete had I known even a fraction of what I had learned within the first year of joining the Regiment, much less what I picked up over the next several years.

One thing that always stood out to me was the fact that a large number of the men in the line units, the ones that did the "heavy lifting" during combat operations were quite young, with many of them only a year or two out of high school. Yet, after going through our training programs, these young Rangers could execute difficult and complex tasks with a level of precision, skill and aggressiveness that was truly impressive. I often wondered what would happen if a high school or college football team consisting of men of the same age as these young Rangers was able to go through our selection and training programs, absorbing our "never quit" *mentality and self- discipline along the way, and was able to return to their league or conference and compete against* "normal" *teams that hadn't done this training. I always believed that the* "Ranger Qualified" *team would have a huge advantage over their competitors, which leads me to the main point that I want to convey to the readers of your book.*

If you are a young athlete that is seeking to achieve high goals, you are going to have to increase your proficiency at various skills and techniques, many of which are going to have to be executed at critical moments of important games or matches. If young men that are only two or three years older than you are right now (assuming that you're in high school) are capable of adopting a "perfect practice" *approach to their training and combine it with high levels of self-discipline and dedication, there's no reason why you can't do the same relative to your own training program. I urge you to reflect upon this thought and ask yourself,* "Why not me, and why not now?"

As a final comment, I want to say that while some observers would say that Rangers train like Olympic athletes, I am of the opinion that Olympic <u>Gold Medalists</u> train like Rangers!"

Now, don't get discouraged or disillusioned regarding the 10,000 hour rule relative to your performance as an athlete. Instead of becoming focused on the 10,000 benchmark itself, focus on the *concept* of continuous study and practice as the most effective path to becoming a high-achiever in your sport.

If you study the individuals that have competed at the Olympic or world-class level in your sport, or those that became professional athletes (played in the NFL, NBA, major league baseball, etc.), you'll probably conclude that they had met and exceeded the 10,000 hour rule during their journey to performing at the highest level of their sport. If you were able to study their athletic careers starting from the time they first entered their sport, you'd probably find that while some of them demonstrated exceptional ability right from the start, most of them experienced the very same type of challenges and setbacks that you have faced or will face in the future. They ultimately achieved greatness by simply putting in the time required to overcome challenges, eliminate weaknesses and become champions.

The good news is that you can do this if you are willing to evaluate your entire approach to your sport and look for ways to sharpen your focus and increase your dedication to getting the most out of your potential as an athlete. It is actually that simple, however it is NOT easy! Are you willing to sacrifice and put in the time required to become the best athlete you can be?

Feedback

Feedback is essential for deliberate practice to be successful. When you are practicing a skill it is imperative that you have your coach or other experienced person watch you so they can tell you what you are doing right or wrong. The person critiquing your practice must be knowledgeable in the sport or activity you are training for. This way they can give you specific guidance on the things you need to work on. Remember, the old saying *"practice makes perfect"* is, in the opinion of most top coaches and trainers, not entirely accurate and most have amended it to read *"perfect practice makes perfect!"* To that point, make sure that whoever is observing you as you practice is capable of evaluating your effort and guiding you toward the attainment of perfection!

Your coaches will play a major role in guiding you as you maneuver your way to excellence. You must keep in mind however, that as you progress and you move up in your expertise level, you must seek out that guidance from people who know more than you do about various aspects of your sport. In fact, you should go out of your way to constantly seek the mentorship or instruction from someone who is willing to challenge you and, when needed, give you painful, honest feedback in order to drive you to a higher level of performance.

One thing you must understand about deliberate practice is that it isn't meant to be fun. It is a systematic and methodical exercise that requires high levels of concentration. For deliberate practice to be successful, you must be willing to challenge yourself by continuously working to improve on your weaknesses. Be prepared to fail often in practice, especially in situations where you are competing with an opponent and trying new techniques. Remember that every failure during deliberate practice of a specific skill will provide you with feedback and information that will ultimately lead to eliminating weaknesses and enhancing your abilities.

Developing Training Routines

The purpose of developing a practice routine is to ensure maximum readiness for competitive events. It is important for all athletes – with the help of their coaches - to develop tailored practice routines for their specific sports. Some of the basic elements of a practice routine are:

Nutrition: When you are preparing for competition, it is imperative that you consciously plan out your meals so that they will provide your body with the fuel, flexibility, and energy that you will need for training and recovery. You must adopt eating habits that routinely provide your body with the best nutrition possible that will allow it to meet the demands you are placing upon it.

Sleep: As mentioned in the Rest and Recovery portion of this book, many studies have shown that there is a direct correlation between the quality and quantity of sleep you get every night and your performance in competitions. You must incorporate planning out your day so that you will allow yourself at least seven-and-a-half to eight hours of sleep per night. Pay attention to your performance, mood and motivation on days when you do get the appropriate amount of sleep and on days when you don't, I guarantee you will see a difference!

Practice: Obviously, the sole purpose of practice is to get yourself ready for actual competition. Every practice session that you conduct should address a specific and practical element of that readiness process. This means that you must conduct all your training practices or workouts with the same level of intensity necessary during a competition. For example: you must always conduct a warm-up prior to a practice session, this includes both a physical and a technical warm-up. You must clear your mind of all diversions and intensify your focus on the task at hand. You must slow or quicken your breathing according to the reactions your body is exhibiting. Use your mental control skills to get yourself to the right mindset and your body to the ideal performance state.

Pre-Competition: Not much should vary in the elements of your training and your pre-competition routines; as I said before: *"Train as you play."* This ties back to the muscle memory development discussed previously. The more you practice something, the more instinctive it becomes. The same goes for your routines. If you make a habit of eating well, sleeping well, conducting your work-outs with intensity, diligently practicing your mental focus and concentration exercises, there will really be very little that you need to be stressed about on *"game day."* Set yourself up so that every aspect of the day falls into place just as you want it. The difference here is the emphasis you assign to your routine on the day of competition. It must be at the forefront of your every move.

Focus Levels: Your focus level is that impenetrable frame of mind that will allow you to perform at an optimal level. There are two types of focus levels: Internal and External. If you have an internal focus style, things you need to do include things like finding a quiet place so you can get yourself to that *"zone"* you need to be in when you compete. The opposite goes for those who have an external focus style. If this is the case, make sure you find a place that provides enough stimuli that you will be able to reach the *"zone"* your way.

Intensity Levels: Depending on your experiences during competitions, you will have figured out what intensity level works better for you. If you know that you perform better when you are relaxed and at a low intensity level, then you must always precede competitions by attaining this physical and mental state. Make sure you give yourself plenty of time to get everything done at a slow pace. If you find that you are rushed or that there is too much commotion around you, simply adjust those elements and get yourself to your appropriate intensity level. Conversely, if you know that the more excitement there is around you the better you perform, make sure you surround yourself with active and enthusiastic people. Don't allow too much time where you are idle, make sure you remain active at all times.

You know yourself better than anyone else, and this means that you are capable of figuring out some of the things that work best as you design your training and your pre-competition routines. Please do not confuse routines with rituals. What I'm talking about here isn't something like wearing the same socks at every game, or touching some item that was designated 'lucky' by someone at some point... These things or rituals serve very little purpose in getting your body and mind ready for a competition, in fact they may detract from it. Your routine must contribute in every way to your readiness effort and have the advantage of being flexible and dynamic.

Perfecting your routines won't be easy, it is simply one of those things that will take time and experience. Eventually you will have a well-established routine that you can depend on to keep you on track to accomplish your objective. By the time that happens, you will have developed your mental focus and your self-awareness and confidence enough that you will be much more independent in conducting your training and practices – you will be able to coach yourself!

Not everyone is fortunate enough to receive the right kind of coaching and guidance at an early age. After reading and understanding the information presented in this chapter you are already a step above some of your peers. Embrace the fact that embarking on the path to truly superior performance is not meant for someone without strong resolve, or for someone who is impatient. Engage in *deliberate practice* — always

147

focusing on tasks beyond your current level of competence and comfort. Above all, if you want to achieve top performance as an athlete, you've got to forget the myths and firmly believe that excellence is achievable for all who are willing to put in the time and effort!

Dealing with Distractions

Intense focus and clarity of thought are two very distinguishable attributes displayed by special operators as they conduct their missions. The ability to maintain focus on the assigned mission, despite any number of distractions that might surface during its execution, is a hallmark of special operators and is a skill that is of obvious value to athletes.

It is a common understanding amongst experienced special operators that *"no battle plan survives the first shot."* In other words, once a combat operation begins, friction and *"fog of war"* often require the men executing it to make rapid decisions and alter the plan to accommodate what is actually happening on the battlefield. To prepare for this, the members of SOF units typically conduct rehearsals of missions, during which various contingency plans and actions are discussed and practiced. These warriors know that it is almost a certainty that something is not going to happen as planned and they adopt an *"expect the unexpected"* attitude that enables them to be agile-minded and decisive during high-stress situations.

149

Unfortunately, many inexperienced athletes do not share this attitude and they spend most of their time thinking about and preparing for competing under ideal conditions. Athletes that are more seasoned have learned that unforeseen situations and various types of distractions frequently occur before and during competitive events. As they gain experience, they develop the ability to maintain their focus despite the unforeseen challenges that occur.

Research has proven that the ability to maintain focus on a task or goal, regardless of distractions, is a proven indicator of success. There is no doubt that the ability to concentrate under pressure and in the face of distractions is critical to any athlete aspiring to success at the highest level of their sport. Experienced coaches and athletes alike understand that among athletes of equal skill and ability, it is, almost always, those with the ability to maintain their composure and ability to focus on the task at hand that emerge as winners.

You will need to train your mind and develop a strong, resilient mindset to go along with your physical training program in order to achieve maximum results as an athlete. The material in this chapter is designed to introduce you to some concepts and techniques that will assist you in developing the champion's mindset that will allow you to effectively cope with distractions.

Internal and External Distractions

In a previous chapter, you learned about internal and external friction and how these conditions can affect the performance of individual special operators as well as the outcome of entire operations. The distractions that athletes will face before and during competition can also be categorized into the same two major types – external and internal. Listed below are some examples of both types of distractions that can be found in most sports.

External Distractions

- Media coverage prior to the event

- The weather

- Conditions in the venue, playing surface, locker room, etc.

- Crowd noise, comments from spectators

- Actions or comments made by your teammates

- Actions or comments made by your opponents

- Problems or issues associated with academics in school

- Comments from coaches, parents, boyfriend or girlfriend, etc.

Internal Distractions

- Inner Critic: It has often been said that you are your own toughest critic, and this can be especially true in the case of young athletes. Unfortunately battling that inner critic will typically drain you of energy and lead to negative thoughts.

Dwelling on these negative thoughts prior to a competition is likely to diminish your level of focus, and therefore have an adverse impact on your performance. The human mind is an amazing thing, but it cannot focus on positive and negative thoughts at the same time. If you focus on positive self-talk and other appropriate thoughts, you can set aside any negative thoughts that are lingering in your mind. Many athletes mentally talk themselves out of performing well prior to an event; don't let this happen to you!

- Focusing on Past Events: Some athletes allow themselves to think about something that has happened to them in the past such as losing a game or match, or making a mistake at a critical moment. They may be facing an opponent that has defeated them in the past, and instead of focusing on the new game plan they are about to execute, they allow themselves to dwell on what happened the last time they faced this particular individual or team. This is obviously not conducive to doing your best at the present moment. In order to successfully overcome this conflict in your mind, you must learn to leave the past in the past. Adopt a mentality of *"what happened... happened. That was then, this is now!"* Remember that at the highest levels, most of the athletes in any sport have been competing against each other for many years. They often have traded wins and losses with these rivals. The main thing to focus on is that on any given day, one athlete can defeat another. The winner is usually the one that is able to clearly focus on the event that is happening now, rather than being distracted by thoughts of what has happened in the past.

- Lack of Confidence: Many athletes, despite having the talent and training necessary to win important competitions and defeat high-level opponents, fail to do so because they lack confidence in one or more aspects of their ability, training and readiness for a particular event. If an athlete has trained and prepared properly, the knowledge of this can be a very powerful confidence builder. Likewise, if an athlete has taken shortcuts and not trained or conditioned properly, he or she knows this and it is easy for them to think negative thoughts that almost guarantee that they will not perform well. Don't let this happen to you! Train well and do everything you can to be fully prepared when it counts; this will enable you to enter a competition with a peaceful state of mind and the ability to focus all of your energy and thoughts on executing the tactics and techniques necessary to win.

Recognizing When Distractions Happen

In order to be able to successfully cope with distractions, you must become aware of them. It may sound a bit strange, but it is a fact that many young athletes aren't fully aware of the fact that they are prone to being distracted before or during competitions. You should reflect on this and assess whether or not you have experienced excessive nervousness, a loss of focus or ability to think clearly about the contest that you are about to engage in or if you actually were distracted to the point that it affected your performance while competing. Try to look for patterns, specific times or situations in which you seem to become distracted. Perhaps it is when one of your parents makes comments about the event, or when your coach speaks with you in the days or hours before competition. It is important that you discover any patterns or routines during which you have become distracted from thinking solely about the competition at hand and the game plan and strategies you and your coaches have already decided upon. Once you recognize when and where you usually become unnerved, lose focus and feel distracted, you can begin to make corrections.

How to Minimize or Defeat Distractions

As mentioned earlier, highly successful athletes demonstrate the ability to maintain their composure and focus during stressful and challenging situations. This ability can be developed and refined over time and you should spend as much time working on it as the physical and technical skills associated with your specific sport. As you train and gain experience in actual competition, you'll find that most of the things which used to distract you and affect your performance no longer bother you. Listed below are a few ways that athletes can make themselves less susceptible to being distracted prior to or during a competition.

Practice and Conditioning: An athlete that experiences excessive fatigue during competition will typically become much less effective from a skill/technique perspective. This type of fatigue could be due to physical over-work, but is probably more related to psychological distress. In other words, an athlete may actually be in superb physical condition, but his or her mental state before or during an event can essentially sap his strength and endurance to the point that it makes it appear that he or she is out of shape. To combat this, athletes should practice their skills and techniques under realistic game-like conditions while they are already tired. If an athlete has a history of fading physically during the late stages of competitions, this type of practice will not only enhance his or her physical capacity, which will probably result in more consistent performances, but it will also provide a huge confidence boost that should not be underestimated. If an athlete is confident that he or she has trained hard under realistic game-like conditions, he or she will know that the *"gas tank"* will be there when it is needed. This type of confidence is very effective in helping an athlete from becoming distracted before or during an event.

Pre-Competition Routines: Athletes at every level participate in individual and team-focused pre-competition routines. The best coaches know that it is important to ensure that any team-focused routines or rituals they institute should not detract team members from effectively engaging in whatever works best for each individual athlete. A pre-competition routine can be a very effective tool to help athletes avoid distractions and maintain focus on an upcoming event. These routines vary greatly from one athlete to another, and experimentation over time can lead an athlete to discover methods that work best for him or her. Remember, the ultimate goal of a pre-competition routine is for an athlete to be relaxed, focused and completely ready to execute the moment his or her event begins.

Relaxation Techniques: In a subsequent chapter, you will learn about the *human stress response*, which is your body's normal and predictable reaction to what your brain perceives as dangerous or stressful situations. Also covered in this chapter are some techniques related to arousal control, such as *visualization* and *positive self-talk*. These techniques and others can help an athlete remain calm and focused, which helps greatly in enabling him or her to avoid being affected by distractions.

If you've ever watched professional and high-level amateur athletes, you probably noticed how calm and relaxed most of them appear to be despite the fact that they are competing in high-stakes events in front of many thousands of screaming fans. There may be television cameras, loud music and many more things that could easily distract these athletes. Yet, it seems that at this level of sport, almost all of these men and women possess the ability to remain calm, focused and capable of ignoring anything that might distract them from thinking about doing what they need to do to win. The material in this chapter and that which you will read in subsequent chapters can help you develop this same kind of inner-peace/focus before and during your own athletic events.

Dealing with Injuries

One of the greatest lessons young athletes can learn from special operators is how to effectively cope with being injured and unable to participate in practice sessions and competitions. The world of special operations is especially demanding on the bodies of the men assigned to these types of units. I think it's redundant to state that special operators have a high likelihood of becoming injured at some point. I think most readers of this book would be quite surprised to learn just how many *"physically broken"* special operators there are within all SOF units.

To a special operator, being injured and incapable of performing his duties, and in some instances, having to remain behind while his teammates are engaging in combat operations, is quite devastating. Being forced to the sidelines can often have a more severe impact on the mental state of an injured operator than the physical injury itself. This will almost always delay the healing process and can ultimately cause additional damage to the psychological well-being of the injured man.

While injured bodies will almost always heal over time, special operators have learned to utilize some proven coping techniques that enable them to mentally adjust to being injured and more importantly, adopt a mindset that is conducive to approaching recovery and rehabilitation in an intelligent, measured and effective manner. These coping methods and techniques also apply to athletes, especially those who are exceptionally dedicated and have a deep love for their sport. In this chapter we will introduce you to some information, concepts and techniques that are utilized by special operators who are injured and desperately want to return to their units in a fully operational status.

The Impact of Being Injured

Like injured special operators, athletes that become physically incapable of participating in their sport face many more challenges than their actual physical injuries. Being forced to the sidelines, even for a short period of time, can be a heavy blow to an athlete, and it can have a negative impact on his or her thoughts, emotions, self-confidence and many aspects of their personal lives.

Special operators and athletes typically react to injuries in a similar manner, often exhibiting a wide range of emotions which may include denial, anger, sadness and in some instances, depression. An injury often seems unfair to anyone who is a vibrant, energetic and active person that enjoys challenging his or her body with rigorous physical activity. Although these feelings and emotions are very real, it is critical, assuming one desires as rapid a recovery as possible, to move beyond the negative and find more positive strategies to cope with this temporary setback. In many cases, learning how to effectively cope with an injury helps an athlete become a more focused, flexible, and resilient competitor.

Coping with the stress of an injury requires both physical and psychological resilience. Because sports injury recovery typically focuses on physical rehabilitation, I'm assuming that anyone reading this book will have access to the appropriate medical care, should they become injured, and that an appropriate rehabilitation plan will be prescribed. However, it is very important to also utilize proven psychological techniques that help athletes recover mentally and emotionally while their bodies are healing.

The 5 Emotional Phases of Injury

During a discussion I had with a psychologist that was working with an Air Force special operations unit, he introduced me to the work of a famed psychologist named Dr. Elizabeth Kubler-Ross, who was considered an authority on human responses to grief. Dr. Kubler-Ross discovered a pattern of predictable psychological responses to negative events and in 1969 she documented them in her book titled *On Death and Dying*. She defined this pattern of psychological responses as 'The Five Stages of Grief', and they are also known as 'The Kubler-Ross model.' The five stages are; Denial, Anger, Bargaining, Depression and Acceptance.

Dr. Kubler-Ross emphasized that not all five stages are necessarily experienced by a person who is grieving over some form of loss or negative event, and the stages do not have to be experienced in the precise order in which she listed them. Notably, her study concluded that there is no guarantee that an individual will ever move on from a given stage, which explains the fact that some people simply never recover from the anger or depression they experience due to a negative event in their lives.

While the Kubler-Ross model was originally designed to illustrate the psychological responses to grief and dying, it is now commonly used to address various types of personal losses or setbacks. It is a fact that special operators that are injured or wounded in some way that causes them to become unable to perform their duties definitely experience all or some of the stages described in the Kubler-Ross model. Sports psychologists also know that an athlete's inability to perform and participate in his or her chosen sport is very likely to evoke these same responses. This is because for many athletes, the training schedule, competitive events and daily interactions with teammates and coaches, comprise a significant and important part of their lives. When this is suddenly and unexpectedly removed due to an injury, many athletes cannot cope. The instinctive response is to deny that there is anything wrong. Additionally, the emphasis placed on certain competitions, tournaments, play-off games, team and individual goals, etc., can be so powerful as to cause an athlete to think they simply must keep going and push through the injury. Naturally, doing so typically only makes things worse and the athlete's injuries worsen in severity.

By now, I am sure you are realizing that as an athlete, the effects of being forced out of action through injury can be as psychologically damaging to you as the physical injury is to your body. The process codified by Dr. Kubler-Ross as the *"five stages of grief"* can be applied to the rehabilitation process following a serious sports injury. For the purpose of this book, the five stages of grief can be applied to dealing with sports injuries as follows:

Denial and Isolation

Accomplished athletes (like most special operators) typically consider themselves to be superior in terms of their physical abilities; and are often unwilling to accept that they could be injured to the degree that they become incapable of competing. This leads to athletes refusing to seek medical treatment or advice, as they attempt to convince themselves that the injury is something akin to a slightly pulled muscle and they'll be able to *"work through it"* over the next few days, etc.

Anger

The sudden realization that an injury has occurred and it is going to keep them on the sidelines predictably leads to athletes being angry at themselves for having allowed the injury to occur. This anger can sometimes result in somewhat irrational behavior, as they blame not only themselves, but their coaches, teammates, opponents, perceived deficiencies in their training program and any number of other factors or issues. Worse, athletes will often question the effectiveness of prescribed treatment methods and may refuse to comply with rehabilitation procedures such as staying off their injured leg, using crutches, etc. This anger and stubborn behavior is the mind's attempt at self-protection and pain-mitigation. Simply put, it is one way an athlete blows off steam once he or she realizes they are injured.

Bargaining

A prescribed lengthy rest period after a sports injury can cause an athlete to feel a certain level of desperation. At this stage, athletes will often try to accelerate their return to competition by attempting to bargain with anyone in a position to change their circumstances. They will plead with their doctors, athletic trainers, coaches, parents, etc. trading their willingness to comply with the required amount of rest/rehabilitation in exchange for being allowed to return to training and competing unrealistically sooner than they should. The athlete typically begins to make bargains with him or herself, saying to themselves things such as, *"if I can rest for two days, the injury will get better,"* or *"I'll just do some light workouts and in a few days, I'll be ready to go."* This is a volatile stage for athletes because they often feel that they know how to best recover and resume competing. They may only comply with certain treatment methods if they are convinced that the procedures will work. Defying the advice of experienced medical doctors, physical therapists will usually result in a best case scenario of recovery being delayed; and worst case scenario the injury will worsen and eventually be irreparable due to lack of proper rest and therapy.

Depression

Like injured special operators who are unable to participate in unit activities, athletes that are sidelined from competition often drift into a state of self-pity and in many instances, they withdraw from their teammates and friends. Due to the fact that the activities related to athletic pursuits often require an athlete to spend great quantities of time either practicing, competing or traveling with their teams and their families, their personal and social interactions revolve mostly around their sports. As a result, the sudden loss of participation in their sport can often cause an athlete to experience a sense of isolation from his or her family, friends, teammates and coaches. At this point, athletes can become so discouraged they can lose hope of ever recovering or being able to recover quickly enough to resume training and competing. They can become depressed and some even decide to quit their sport entirely.

Acceptance

At some point, most athletes realize that they are indeed injured and incapable of effectively or safely participating in their sport. This mental state of acceptance enables athletes to stop dwelling on the fact that they are sidelined from competing and sharpens their focus on the rehabilitation program or processes prescribed by medical professionals. Once this happens, an athlete typically begins to feel a sense of accomplishment; and even though it may be slight, that progress is being made and it is only a matter of time before they can resume competing.

Strategies for Injured Athletes

When an injury occurs there are some things that you can do to lessen the impact it may have on your overall well-being and fitness.

Managing Emotional and Physical Effects of an Injury

There is no way to predict how much time an athlete may spend at each of the 5 phases; it all really depends on each individual's qualities. As previously discussed, a typical athlete will need approximately10 years or 10,000 hours of training and practice in order to reach what is typically considered an expert level in his or her sport. So, in the grand scheme of things, taking a few weeks off to heal an injury won't have much of an impact on your performance several years down the road. As long as young athletes have already decided to commit themselves to ultimately reaching that expert level, their perspective will be much different when they look at what an injury means. Once that ultimate goal is established, the athlete will know and accept that becoming injured is more than likely going to be part of the journey. This clearer and more focused perspective will aid athletes as they assume control over the recovery process and work with the medical teams and coaches to ensure proper healing. Awareness of the fact that there will also be some emotional and psychological effects that go along with an injury will allow athletes and coaches to be more prepared to deal with them. This different perspective will also help with how you view injuries and therefore also change how you feel about them. They will no longer be a source of great anxiety or stress, but rather another routine to incorporate into your practice.

Learning About Your Injury

It is important that you try to learn as much as you can about the injury you are dealing with. Knowing what led to the injury, how to prevent it in the future, and what the treatment entails will allow you to be better equipped to talk to the medical personnel in charge of your case. It will also diminish the amount of anxiety you may feel about what the injury really means.

Some questions you may ask your doctors, coaches and athletic trainers in order to make sure you clearly understand your situation are:

- What is my diagnosis (what type of injury do I have)?
- How long will recovery take?
- How do the treatments I'm receiving help with the healing?
- What will my rehabilitation entail?
- Are there any exercises or alternative workouts I can do?

I would also encourage you to conduct your own basic research. There is plenty of information available online that you can easily access in order to gain a basic understanding of what your body is going through. Remember however, that the purpose is to gain a better understanding of things, not so that you can self-diagnose! Just learning the basic physiology behind how the injured part of your body works will give you a greater sense of control as you work toward recovery.

Maintaining a Positive Attitude

Although it may be quite difficult for most athletes, it is absolutely imperative to stay positive as you work on rehabilitation. A good way to do this is to approach your therapy and rehab as you would while training for an important competition. You need to focus on the task and the requirements and actions needed to successfully accomplish the task. If the therapy for an injured shoulder calls for lifting just one pound of weight, then focus on the exact movement and the exact muscles that you are trying to heal. If you approach rehab this way, you will also implement all the other elements of deliberate practice that we discussed earlier. It is also very important to use positive self-talk as you undergo rehabilitative exercises. Don't dwell on the fact that you are hurt and can't do things as you're used to; instead focus on the fact that every therapy brings you closer to your goal of getting back to the sport you love.

Using Your Support Network

Although you might feel as though you can't be a part of things with your team as you work on your recovery, it is very important that you not isolate yourself from your team. Your coach, your teammates, parents and friends are an important part of the recovery process. They, better than most, will be more understanding if you need to vent or talk about your frustrations. They will know where you're coming from and can offer different perspectives that may help you through the tough days. Also realize that you can set an example for your teammates to follow as to how to handle yourself after an injury. So, stay connected to the team, attend practice even if you can't fully participate. Remember you are part of a team; they can help you as much as you can help them!

Focusing on Milestones

Just as with the goals you set for training, you will now set new goals that focus on recovery rather than performance. As you achieve these milestones in your recovery, you will feel a sense of accomplishment and remain positive and motivated. Unlike training and practice sessions, where it is important for an athlete to push past some limitations, during recovery from an injury it is important to know not to push too fast or too hard or you may actually cause more damage to your body. Working closely with your doctors, athletic trainers and coaches will help you set realistic and effective goals that will ensure your injury heals properly.

Overcoming an injury without allowing it to derail your athletic endeavors is not impossible. It does take a change in perspective, some research and learning, and of course, a lot of patience. Your world does not have to be turned upside down due to an injury; you simply need to refocus your efforts from training to compete, to training toward healing and recovering to be able to compete. Don't forget to reach out to people around you who care for you and are willing to stand by you as you go through the ups and the downs of recovery. Use all the resources you have at your disposal to gain knowledge, design a recovery plan and stay fit while recovering. Injuries, for most athletes, are simply part of the journey!

Mental Toughness

Although there are many definitions of what being 'mentally tough' means, I think, for our purposes, *mental toughness* can be defined as that fundamental block upon which all other qualities and competencies associated with special operators are built. I think this also applies to high-performing athletes. Assuming that you have set lofty goals as an athlete, you will inevitably have to compete against the most highly skilled competitors in your sport. To get to that point, where you're able to compete against the best of the best, you will need to endure, in most cases, an extensive training and development plan that will require you to demonstrate an exceptional level of commitment. This quality comes from deep within you; some call it guts, or heart, or grit; but for the purposes of this book and subsequent discussions, we'll refer to it as *mental toughness*.

I think that if you ask any number of people for their definition of mental toughness, you'd get many different answers. This is exactly what happens even among members of various SOF units; they all know what it is they are trying to describe, yet there is no common definition for it in the special operations community, at least, none that I am aware of.

A highly-regarded sports psychologist, Dr. Jim Loehr of the Human Performance Institute defined mental toughness as follows:

> *"Mental toughness is the ability to consistently perform towards the upper range of your talent and skill regardless of competitive circumstances. It is all about improving your mind so that it's always on your side; not sometimes helping you nor working against you as we all know it's quite capable of doing."*

In a research paper titled "What Is This Thing Called Mental Toughness? An Investigation of Elite Sport Performers," authors Graham Jones, Sheldon Hanton and Declan Connaughton declared that mental toughness is *"Having the natural or developed psychological edge that enables you to: generally, cope better than your opponents with the many demands (competition, training, lifestyle) that sport places on a performer; specifically, be more consistent and better than your opponents in remaining determined, focused, confident, and in control under pressure."*

In my opinion, it is a common misconception to think that mental toughness is an innate quality that some people are simply born with – you either have it or you don't. I believe that mental toughness can be learned and developed by anyone who is determined and passionate about a specific goal. Mental toughness is a key trait that you need in order to be able to overcome any obstacle that stands between you and your success in achieving a set goal. It means being able to remain focused and determined until you complete a task, regardless of difficulties encountered along the way.

Almost every special operator that I've ever spoken with on the topic of SOF selection courses and the men that make the cut and those that do not, emphasize that ultimately, what determines whether or not a man is successful depends upon him winning the battle that is constantly raging inside his mind and presents the question *"How much do I really want this?"* Every special operator I know has told me stories of men that had experienced setbacks during selection (injuries, academic issues, personal issues such as the death of a family member, personality clashes with instructors, etc.) that would cause most men to quit. Yet, the men they describe did not quit, instead, they simply refused to acknowledge the possibility of defeat and in many instances, seemed to actually become stronger mentally as the level of adversity or stress intensified.

Mental toughness is normally associated with physically demanding professions such as the military, professional sports, world class amateur athletics, etc. In extremely physically demanding fields such as special operations, mental toughness is typically evaluated and developed by exposing men to prolonged and exhausting periods of physical training. These training evolutions contain various activities that place emphasis on heightening levels of endurance and ability to cope with stress, pain and suffering. This is appropriate because of the real-world demands placed on military personnel, it is critical that they be pushed to their physical limits in order to replicate the stress levels associated with combat situations. This type of physical rigor can also be useful for athletes, assuming that these conditions are practiced in a safe, controlled environment that is supervised by competent coaches and athletic trainers.

Like their special operator counterparts, high-level athletes must also consistently demonstrate the ability to remain composed, confident and focused during tournaments or competitions. I think we can all agree that in order to perform well as an athlete, you must possess a certain type of mental toughness and emotional control that enables you to process fear and anxiety as the levels of competition increase. It is through constant practice and training that this level of control can be developed. There are some elements that have been identified as the basis of mental toughness, and that you can use in order to cultivate it within yourself.

What Special Operators Say About Mental Toughness

During my research for this book, I became aware of a study that was done by a member of a SOF unit on the topic of mental toughness and the long-term success of individual special operators. The population that was tested and evaluated in this study consisted of several dozen operators representing every major unit in the special operations community.

During this research, special operators were asked to provide their personal definition for the term *mental toughness*. The results are shown below and I think you'll find them quite interesting. While reading them, ask yourself which statements align with what you already believe about mental toughness and which are new; and how this information might apply to your outlook and philosophies regarding your goals and aspirations as an athlete. It is important that you remember that the comments seen below were made by active-duty special operators, most of whom were combat veterans. Their experiences naturally resulted in them mentioning combat operations and, in some cases, the loss of teammates during battle.

As an athlete, you are not likely to encounter life-threatening situations while training and competing; but you can gain a lot of benefit from the comments seen below if you reflect upon them and, when possible, apply them to your specific sport and your current mindset as an athlete.

Special Operator Comments on Mental Toughness:

- Having unshakable confidence in your ability to achieve your goals.

- Knowing that you possess unique qualities and abilities that make you better than your opponents.

- Having an insatiable desire to succeed.

- Being resilient and able to quickly recover from adversity, disappointment, set-backs, etc.

- Thriving on the pressure of high-stakes events, including combat operations.

- Accepting that fear and anxiety are inevitable and knowing that you can overcome both.

- Able to remain fully focused on the mission.

- Remaining fully focused on the task at hand in the face of life-threatening situations.

- Being able to cope with high levels of physical and emotional pain, while still maintaining the ability to execute skills and tasks required to accomplish the mission.

- Quickly regaining psychological control following unexpected, uncontrollable events such as the death of a unit member during combat.

Traits Specific to Mental Toughness

You should note that the traits of motivation, confidence, focus, composure and resilience emerged as common denominators among the responses given by the men being interviewed. I don't think this will come as a surprise to most readers. I think most already understand that to perform effectively as a member of a special operations unit, men must possess a certain type of mental toughness and emotional control that enables them to cope with fear and anxiety during combat operations. I think most also assume that these men receive training that ultimately enables them to remain composed, confident and focused during the most difficult and dangerous situations imaginable. Let's discuss each of the five traits mentioned above in more detail.

Motivation

Any goal we set for ourselves has finality to it; there is an end-state that we are looking to achieve. Keeping this end-state in focus is in itself the motivator that will keep you moving toward it. This component of mental toughness is perhaps the most important one, because even if you possess the other four in ample amounts, they won't do you any good if you're not motivated to take action! I recommend that you ask yourself *"Why am I doing this?"* or *"Why is it important that I achieve this goal?"* This will enable you to better understand your motivations and desires, which can lead to enhanced focus and more clearly stated goals.

Confidence

Confidence is a critical ingredient to mental toughness. It enables you to know that you have the skills and knowledge to achieve the challenge or task facing you, and it also enables you to bounce back after setbacks, mistakes or poor performances. Special operators typically have an unshakeable confidence in their abilities. This comes from the fact that they have confidence in their skills and *"game plan,"* and in their ability to execute the plan during stressful, high-pressure situations. A good way to develop this trait is through repeatedly practicing whatever skill you would like to master. As an athlete, knowing that you've put in the time and practice required to become highly skilled in various aspects of your sport is a great confidence builder.

Focus

The ability to focus – to home in on what's most important at a given time – and to be able to block out everything else, is a huge factor in the development of mental toughness. For centuries, soldiers have talked about the *"Fog of War"* that occurs during battles, and how one must consciously remain focused on the mission and avoid being distracted or confused by irrelevant or insignificant issues. Some special operators refer to this as *"being in the zone."* It implies a state of *hyper-focus* on what's most important at a given moment to accomplish the mission. I'm sure you can see the value of this trait as it relates to your performance as an athlete.

Composure

In order to perform at your maximum potential as an athlete, you must be able to remain composed and in control during the most stressful competitive situations. Doing so enables you to have clarity and focus during the heat of battle, and it promotes sound decision-making. Composure is all about your mind being in control of the emotions and reactions that are being produced by your brain's automatic responses to certain situations. Knowing these responses will occur enables you to cope with them by overriding your brain's signals with those being sent by your well-trained mind.

Hopefully, you are starting to understand that <u>the brain and mind are two separate things</u>. Your body obeys the brain, but the brain obeys the mind! The men that attend various SOF selection courses are constantly confronted with situations that require them to use their minds (mental toughness) to overcome what their brains are telling their bodies. Their brains tell them that they are too tired, too cold or hot, that they are injured and can't possibly pass the next graded event, etc. Many of these men, the vast majority in fact, succumb to how their brains react and they voluntarily quit. Those able to use their minds to remain composed, focus on the task at hand and simply do the very best they can at that moment. They use their minds to reach deep within themselves and find the strength to hang on and keep moving forward.

As an athlete, you will surely encounter situations during practice or actual competitions where your brain will tell you that you are just too tired to execute proper techniques and skills, or that there's no way you can come from behind to win a game, match or whatever event you're competing in. It is up to your mind to remain in control and push you to stay focused until you have overcome the obstacles facing you.

Resilience

Resilience is a critical factor of being successful as a special operator and as an athlete. This trait is typically one of the most heavily discussed whenever the topic of mental toughness is being debated. Like the young men striving to gut their way through the various special operations training pipelines, you will surely face obstacles and setbacks while you work toward accomplishing your goals. Resilience is the quality that enables people to bounce back from these challenges and get back on the path to success. It is a quality that you must seek to develop if you aspire to high-achievement as an athlete.

Mental Toughness for Life

Mental toughness is a skill that, once developed in yourself for athletic purposes, can continue to be of benefit throughout all stages of your life. Even in professions where very little physical exertion or physical strength and fitness are ever required, mental toughness plays a very important role in achieving success. Additionally, people undergoing any kind of *"personal battle"* - such as difficult situations at work; dealing with family or personal relationship problems; coping with health issues, depression, drug addiction, alcoholism or obesity - need a great amount of mental toughness in order to push past limitations, deal with the challenges facing them, and follow whatever steps are necessary to achieve their goals.

In summary, mental toughness is a quality that is critical to maximizing your potential as an athlete. The most important thing to remember is that mental toughness can, in fact, be studied, developed, practiced and mastered!

Fear and Stress

The education and training associated with producing special operators is very costly; not only financially expensive, but also incredibly time consuming and lengthy. It takes several years to train individuals to the level of proficiency needed to accomplish the various difficult and dangerous missions that SOF units participate in. As mentioned in a previous chapter, leaders within the special operations community have become much more proactive in trying to ensure that the highly-trained members of their units remain healthy, physically fit and available for world-wide operations on short notice.

You've read about the many advances that have been made in recent years that have led to the adoption of advanced physical training and sports medicine techniques by trainers within SOF units. You should also know that during the past several years much more attention had been given to the study of various methods and techniques that are focused on the psychological well-being of special operators and the development of a mindset that enables these men to consistently perform well under some of the most dangerous and stressful conditions imaginable.

The material in this chapter will provide readers with an understanding of some of the measures that are taken to develop, refine and maintain this mindset. Although there are many different programs and tools used by the various SOF units to promote this mindset among individual operators, one commonality among these programs and tools is that they all seek to enable the individual with an enhanced understanding of, and ability to effectively cope with what is referred to as the *human stress response*.

Additionally, all of these programs are based upon the premise that special operators with greater tenure are at greater risk of experiencing the negative impact of the *cumulative stress* associated with nearly continuous exposure to situations that elicit the human stress response. Both factors, the human stress response and the effects of cumulative stress, can also have a huge impact on the performance and long-term well-being of athletes. I believe that the methods used by special operators to cope with these issues can be very effective if used appropriately by athletes.

The Human Stress Response

Technology has dramatically changed the nature of warfare during the past several centuries, but one thing remains constant, today's warriors react to the stresses of combat, especially that which brings about fear, in the same way that our club-, spear- and sword-wielding ancestors did. No amount of technology has been able to change the fact that men engaged in combat operations, or other high risk activities, still have to face the fear of death or injury. It is obvious that fear can affect an individual to the point that he fails in combat. Knowing this, the armed forces in general, and the special operations community in particular, has devoted much time and resources to studying this issue in an attempt to develop methods that will enable warriors to overcome their primal responses to stressful situations. A good amount of the knowledge gained from this research can be leveraged by athletes, since their bodies and brains also react in the same predictable manner when exposed to situations that elicit significant stressors.

To operate effectively in combat situations, special operators must be able to remain focused as they operate highly technical equipment, make rapid decisions and execute physical tasks that require both fine and gross motor skills, often while being hunted or shot at by a determined enemy. Success depends on a mind that is conditioned to expect fear and knows how to neutralize its impact on human performance. When asked about the topic of fear, one highly experienced special operator told me that in his opinion, there are two kinds of combat soldiers, those who admitted they'd felt fear and those who were lying! He went on to state that:

"Special operators are human and all humans are vulnerable to feeling fear. It is their training that enables them to control their reactions to dangerous situations in a way that untrained individuals cannot."

The Physiology of Fear

To learn how to control fear, you must first understand your body's natural response to it. Fear stimulates the sympathetic nervous system, which is responsible for the *"fight or flight"* response that is programmed into our brains as a result of millions of years of human evolution. This response has been present since the first cavemen fought with each other over food, or when they faced off against an animal that was trying to kill them! The famed Prussian General Carl Von Clausewitz described the human response to fear in this way:

"The fog of war can prevent the enemy from being seen, a gun from firing when it should, a report from reaching a commander."

This response can cause men in combat to lose the ability to perform the simplest of tasks (reloading their weapon, etc.) and to become physically weak to the point that they cannot remain standing, or muster the strength to operate equipment or perform tasks that they've done successfully hundreds or thousands of times in the past.

When the brain registers a situation that induces fear, it begins a chemical reaction in our bodies, sometimes referred to as the *"fight-or-flight"* reaction. The first thing that happens is an almost immediate release of a hormone called adrenaline (also known as the fight-or-flight hormone). Imagine you are driving along, and suddenly the car in the lane next to you starts to change lanes and cuts you off, you have to slam on your breaks to avoid being hit. When it's all over and you've stopped honking your horn at the driver, you will notice that your heart is pounding; you're breaking into a sweat and you are breathing really fast.

All these reactions in your body are the result of adrenaline having been released into your bloodstream. Adrenaline also causes a surge of energy or *"arousal."* Almost at the same time as adrenaline is released, the adrenal glands also release another hormone called norepinephrine. What this hormone does is make you more aware, more awake and able to react. It also shifts the blood flow from areas that may not be quite as necessary, like the skin, to others, like your muscles, which would be essential for fleeing from danger. This is why you would probably feel a tingly feeling all over your body after a close-call-type event.

Finally, we have a chemical chain-reaction, which takes a few minutes, and that results in the release of cortisol into the blood. Cortisol regulates the fluid flow and the blood pressure in our bodies. All of the following reactions occur in our bodies as a response to fear or stress:

- Increased heart rate and breathing: Your body is trying to get more oxygen to larger muscle groups in order to get them ready for action.

- Butterflies: As the oxygen is diverted to other muscles, the abdominal area is being deprived of oxygen, which causes a fluttering sensation.

- Sweating: The sudden surge of blood flow to large muscle groups generates more heat; your body is attempting to regulate it through sweating.

- Shaking: The blood flow is being rerouted to the major muscle groups so fine motor skills become compromised, which causes tremors and shaking. This condition is also known as *"the jitters"* and you've probably already experienced it to some degree during your athletic career.

- Dizziness: Increased rate of breathing can often cause a level of hyperventilation, which can flood the brain with too much oxygen, causing dizziness.

- Dry mouth: There are several physiological reasons for this, but the main ones are that the increased rate of breathing has a *"drying"* effect on the mouth and throat area.

- Dilated pupils: Blood flow is increased to the eyes, causing the pupils to dilate and better enabling the person to see potential threats.

- Slurred speech: Blood flow is diverted away from areas of the brain associated with secondary functions such as speech, and this often causes a person to slur his words and speak at a slower rate than normal.

How to Control Fear

The first step in controlling fear is to recognize the predictable and normal physiological effects produced by the human stress response. The ability to recognize these physical effects and neutralize them is the key to maintaining a focused state of mind during periods of great stress, which of course, enables a person to perform at desired levels.

When a situation or event occurs, whether it's something unforeseen or a scheduled event such as a competition or tournament, there are a few processes that take place. First we analyze or appraise the situation and the burden it is placing on us, then we assess how equipped we are to deal with the situation and, finally, we judge the ramifications or consequences we would face if we failed or succeeded in handling the situation. All of these processes occur almost instantaneously, in fractions of a second. After the processes have been concluded and our assessment has taken place, then the physiological responses to fear occur.

Although we normally think of our feelings or emotions as a direct result of a situation, it is important to understand that that isn't quite correct. It isn't the situation that causes the emotional reaction; it is the interpretation or assessment that our *"mind"* gives to the situation. It all depends on whether the mind perceives that the individual is capable of coping with the situation or not.

186

Untrained individuals often believe that raw courage is all that is necessary to defeat fear and its effects, and many special operators were once included in this group. As a result of research on this topic, SOF leaders now know that it is critical that every special operator understands the physical and emotional causes of fear and be able to identify situations in which the body will begin reacting to it. If one is able to anticipate situations that will initiate the body's coping mechanism for fear (the physiological responses listed above), the proper steps can be taken to thwart these bodily reactions and maintain lower heart rates and, in turn, the ability to perform assigned tasks. Although impossible to eradicate completely, fear can be effectively controlled to maximize performance under the most stressful of situations. Obviously, this is something that would be of great benefit to any athlete aspiring to compete at the highest levels of his or her sport.

Of major importance when trying to control fear is for the individual to understand that it is a normal occurrence; feeling it does not mean one is a coward or in some way *"lacking guts."* Openly discussing fear should be encouraged; it should be thought of as yet another challenge to be tackled. One scientific study showed that eight out of ten combat veterans felt that it is better to admit fear and discuss it openly before battle. The belief that *"the man who knows he will be afraid and tries to get ready for it makes a better soldier,"* was shared by 58 percent of those surveyed.

187

Openly discussing fear has never been easy for special operators. Because they are almost all driven, Type-A personalities, used to overcoming significant obstacles and performing much better than most *"normal"* men, the members of SOF units are often reluctant to admit that they have any weaknesses, even those that they were born with as a result of human evolution! The good news is that the leadership within the SOF community recognized that utilizing the information gained from various studies could enable them to enhance the performance of their operators, and most special operators now have access to psychologists and other medical professionals that are focused on helping them maintain a strong, resilient mindset over the course of their careers in SOF units.

Every SOF unit has adopted certain methods and techniques that enable their operators to adequately address the human stress response. Some of these are classified and cannot be shared with the public, but thankfully, a good amount of this knowledge is available and has been presented in this chapter. In particular, the Naval Special Warfare community has freely shared extensive amounts of information regarding how Navy SEALs are trained to address their reactions to the human stress response. While I am sure they haven't shared everything they know, for obvious reasons, what they have shared is quite informative and can be of great value to athletes that aspire to high-achievement. As you read the following material, contemplate how the situations, reactions and techniques described apply to your role as an athlete and how you might integrate some of this knowledge into your training program.

Navy SEALs and the Human Stress Response

Students at the Navy SEAL training and selection course, known as BUD/S, are taught to utilize seven techniques as a way of maintaining their resolve and motivation in the face of stress and fear, and as a way of recovering mentally after these situations. BUD/S students and fully-qualified SEALs are now trained to understand that the body's reactions to fear, or the human stress response, are as normal and predictable as the body's reactions to holding your breath underwater for a prolonged period, or when the body is subjected to prolonged cold that leads to hypothermia. SEALS now understand that what used to be attributed solely to *"guts"* is actually a man's ability to use his mind to anticipate and identify any situation that will trigger one or more of the body's physical responses to fear and to counter these responses very early, enabling them to remain calm and effective on the battlefield.

Because the SEALS have always engaged in very challenging and realistic training, it was very easy for them to incorporate the concept of *"controlling fear"* into it. SEALs are constantly exposed to training that replicates the tempo, stress and physical and mental demands of actual combat situations (as are members of all SOF units), which provides them with almost unlimited opportunities to practice utilizing these techniques to control their body's response to fear or threat stress. By now, these techniques are so well known and have proven so effective that they have become part of the individual SEAL's *"tool box,"* according to one Navy psychologist that was involved in the process of integrating them into SEAL training and development programs.

The Seven Techniques

1. Goal Setting and Segmenting

When Navy psychologists conducted studies to identify why so many BUD/S candidates failed to make it through training, they found that many of the students that failed, or voluntarily dropped out of the course, admitted that they allowed themselves to become consumed with thoughts about how much training they had ahead of them. Knowing that the vast majority of men did not typically graduate from the course, and that they had so many training events and tests ahead of them, they felt overwhelmed to the point they considered their goal of becoming a Navy SEAL to be a lost cause. Their negative thoughts resulted in poor performance that led to their dismissal from the course, or they simply quit and gave up on their dream. The researchers also discovered that almost all candidates that had successfully completed the course and then went on to serve as SEALs had used a technique in which they established short-term, mid-term, and long-term goals for themselves throughout BUD/S and the many months of follow-on training. This technique is referred to as segmenting and it essentially breaks down larger goals into smaller and more manageable pieces or phases.

What this means is that instead of dwelling on the fact that they were facing many weeks of training ahead of them, most successful trainees would instead focus on that specific training day and further segment the day into several stages. This technique is sometimes referred to as *"chunking"* or, as some would say *"eating an elephant one bite at a time."*

Rather than focusing on the knowledge that it would be a very tough day full of several difficult events, trainees would instead focus on making it through the early morning physical training session. During this session, they'd think of nothing but the specific exercise they were doing at the time. Then their complete focus would go to the next exercise dictated by the instructor, and then the next one after that. Once physical training was over, the next segment of the day would be to get cleaned up and make sure their barracks rooms were ready for inspection. Once the room inspection was completed, the class would run to a classroom for several periods of instruction.

During this period of several hours, the trainees would focus only on the class being taught. After the classes were completed, the trainees would be directed to the obstacle course for a *"timed run,"* which many trainees found quite challenging and stressful due to the rather severe consequences if they failed to meet the time requirements. This event typically weighs heavily on the minds of many BUD/S trainees; and those that allow themselves to dwell on it during earlier portions of the day, often lose focus during the preceding training evolutions, which could cause them to fail or otherwise incur the wrath of the instructors. In some instances they would become so anxious and nervous about the timed run of the obstacle course, that their energy and concentration were greatly diminished, which in turn resulted in poor performance during this graded event.

By focusing on each segment of the day – what they were currently tasked with doing – successful BUD/S trainees avoided focusing on the rather dreadful fact that they had many months of exceptionally difficult training ahead. They segmented the grueling six-month course into months, weeks, days and then each day into several *"chunks"* of time and they focused on successfully completing them one at a time.

Goal setting and segmentation are time-tested techniques that you should consider utilizing in your training program. There are many commonalities with trainees attempting to make it through the long and arduous training programs associated with special operations units and athletes training before, during and after their competitive season.

2. *Arousal Control*

As discussed above, when a person is exposed to stressful situations that trigger the human stress response, his or her brain will automatically initiate a chemical reaction that will produce almost immediate effects on certain bodily functions and a range of emotions. This arousal response is a perfectly normal and predictable reaction by human beings, but it can also have a negative impact on a person's critical thinking, decision making, and fine motor skills.

For special operators, allowing themselves to become negatively affected by emotions such as anger, fear or anxiety is not conducive to combat effectiveness. The need for arousal control is paramount in high-stake situations; and many special operators use some form of deep-breathing technique to help them stay calm and focused on their objective. This topic will be discussed in more detail in the following chapter.

3. *Visualization*

Visualization is a technique that has been used by athletes for many years. SOF units have gradually increased its use over the past decade or so. One of the goals of visualization is to essentially combat fear and stress in difficult situations. Operators visualize in their minds events that may take place during an upcoming combat operation, mission or attack. They try to predict how they will react to various elements; what tactics or actions they will need to employ given certain changes or unforeseen events. Not only do they visualize what they might see, but also what they might hear or even smell. Repetition of this exercise will enable an operator to be prepared with a plan of action for the various scenarios that may present themselves. In this way, when an operator actually faces the situation, though it may be the first time he is physically engaged in it, in his mind he has already gone over it numerous times. This state of readiness in his mind serves to preempt the stress responses that would arise otherwise.

For example, during BUD/S training, students, wearing SCUBA gear and submerged under water, are required to correctly execute various emergency procedures and corrective actions to resolve problems with their equipment. This exercise is considered by many BUD/S students to be among the most mentally challenging tests they take during their training. During this evolution the instructors will attack the students and snatch the regulators from their mouths, close SCUBA-tank air valves, disconnect hoses from the tanks, tie the hoses in knots, and other such things. Most of the students are still very new to being underwater and wearing SCUBA gear; and they are not yet completely comfortable and confident in this environment. Adding to the mental stress of this evolution is the fact that if a student panics and surfaces without permission he fails the event. If he performs the proper corrective actions too fast or too slow, he will also be deemed a failure. If the instructors feel he didn't appear confident and relaxed while executing the corrective actions, they will also fail the student. If he fails to pass the evolution after a few attempts, he will be recycled to another BUD/S class or in some instances, removed from the course.

Navy psychologists found that a majority of the successful students had experienced a significant degree of anxiety and apprehension for this training evolution given its difficulty. However, they also found that almost all of the students that successfully completed this evolution on the first attempt had utilized a technique in which they visualized themselves going through the various emergency actions they'd been taught and would be tested on. They knew exactly what to do to remedy all situations and problems the instructors could possibly impose upon them; and they repeatedly went through these actions in their mind in the days and hours prior to the actual test. They mentally rehearsed being attacked from the rear by two or more instructors who would snatch the masks from their faces and regulators from their mouths or would remove the scuba tanks from their bodies. As a result of this visualization, once the evolution was actually underway, the students were able to ignore the fact that they were being attacked and focused entirely on calmly solving the problems being presented to them.

Visualization and mental-rehearsal techniques have been used for many years by people in various professions and sports that are associated with high-risk/high-stress situations. Chances are that you have already engaged in some degree of visualization prior to competitive events. I recommend that you formalize your use of this technique to the degree that you literally visualize your next competition from the moment you arrive at the venue it will be played at, through your warm-ups and the actual competition itself. Using this technique not only provides your mind the opportunity to engage in a series of rehearsals, it also sharpens your focus and helps you avoid distractions prior to and during the competition.

4. *Positive Self-Talk*

Psychologists have long known how important positive self-talk can be for any individual. They know how much of a positive impact it can have on a person as they undergo periods of great stress or anxiety; or when they are engaged in the pursuit of a significant and highly desired personal or professional goal, objective, prize, achievement, or form of recognition. One highly-regarded psychologist with extensive experience working with special operators has stated that he believes the self-talk technique to be the most important and effective action an individual can engage in in order to develop a strong, confident and resilient mindset.

Research studies have shown that the average person thinks at a rate of 1,000 to 5,000 words per minute. Even when a person is alone, sitting silently, there is an active *"conversation"* taking place within his or her mind. Common sense would tell us that the more positive and upbeat these conversations are, the more beneficial they would be toward a person's outlook, attitude, and feelings regarding any aspect of their life. In other words, we are in complete control of the conversations that are taking place within our minds, and we should ensure that they are of a positive nature. Reflect upon the *"conversations"* you've had with yourself prior to, during and after competitive events and you'll probably realize that your performance was directly affected, positively or negatively, by your state of mind and what you were thinking.

Young men that are going through the various SOF selection courses are constantly faced with tests and graded evolutions of ever-increasing difficulty. The stakes are quite high; if they do not achieve a passing grade, they will not realize their dream of serving in a SOF unit. A student in any of these courses will 'talk to himself' hundreds of times per day. He reminds himself that all of the pain he's enduring is the price to pay to achieve his goal of becoming a special operator and that nothing, no amount of pain, will cause him to fail to achieve his goal. Formal studies of special operators show that there is a very high correlation of successfully completing a SOF selection course and an individual student's ability to engage in continuous, positive self-talk throughout the course. Seasoned special operators also engage in positive self-talk throughout their careers as they repeatedly participate in very stressful and dangerous training and real-world operations.

As an athlete, you'd be wise to adopt and refine the use of the self-talk technique. It is perhaps the single most valuable tool that you can use to develop the mindset, confidence and resilience needed to achieve your goals.

5. *Compartmentalization*

The grim reality of warfare means that special operators will inevitably experience various types of emotions. All combat soldiers are taught to expect casualties within their units once actual combat begins. Seeing comrades, some of whom are close personal friends, seriously wounded or killed can produce various reactions such as sadness, anger and, of course, fear. During such situations, it is imperative that they continue to focus on the mission and not allow their emotions to distract or deter them from executing their specific roles. Essentially, these men are taught to temporarily suspend their natural reactions to fear and the death and destruction that are often associated with combat operations. They learn to suppress normal human responses to extreme stress during the actual fight, knowing that they'll be able to address their emotions, the loss of friends, etc., at a later time, when it is safe to do so.

Fortunately, for you, it is unlikely that you will witness or experience something this traumatic during your training or competitions. However, the technique of compartmentalization can be very effective for athletes before, during and after a competitive event. For instance, if an athlete experiences a setback during an early portion of competition, he or she must be able to *"shake it off"* and focus on scoring points or whatever it is that will achieve victory. There are numerous examples of individual athletes and teams that could not mentally overcome setbacks, unexpected situations, being scored upon, etc., and were unable to regain focus during the competition. Often, these individuals or teams become so *"rattled"* that they rapidly *"self-destruct"* and perform terribly. Of course, there are also countless examples of individuals and teams that did just the opposite, and were able to come back from early setbacks and win the competition. There is a time and a place for everything; and during a competition is the time to maintain complete focus on the execution of your techniques and skills. It is imperative that you learn how to completely block out everything else.

6. *Contingency Planning*

Another technique used to minimize an individual's response to stress is contingency planning. This technique is closely aligned with visualization. In preparation for upcoming missions, special operators will dissect the entire operation from start to finish; discussing what the plan is as well as all alternate actions that will be necessary if, for various reasons, the plan becomes untenable and rapid adjustments need to be made in order to achieve success. The main benefit of doing contingency planning is that the special operators are acknowledging up front that the plan will probably not be executed flawlessly, and while doing so, they can individually and collectively prepare for what may happen at various stages of the operation, and decide on what actions they will take in advance. As a result, they are typically able to adjust the battle plan with little or no hesitation during critical phases of an operation, when lives are at stake and momentum must be maintained.

Interestingly, many coaches do not want their athletes to engage in contingency planning prior to an event. They prefer their athletes to think only positive thoughts and to visualize the *"perfect game"* and to psych themselves up to the point they believe that things are going to go exactly as planned during the event. While I am sure this works for some athletes, I recommend that you avoid this approach to competition. Just as special operators know that *"no battle plan survives the first shot,"* you probably already know that your competitions rarely proceed exactly as planned. Instead of visualizing perfection, I think you should focus on visualizing reality. Thinking about what can happen during an event, and knowing that you have already thought about what actions you will take is a very powerful confidence builder. This confidence also enables rapid reaction to an obstacle or setback, which in turn enables you to avoid your body's normal response to stressors. Simply put, it's not about what happens during a competition, it's what you do in response to what happens that counts. Engaging in contingency planning is a superb way to enhance your chances of success!

7. Focus and Concentration

Special operators engage in very dangerous training and real-world operations. Operating in continuous high-stress/high risk environments requires a great amount of focus and concentration from each individual involved. If an operator lacks focus or is unable to concentrate on the task at hand, inevitably his performance will deteriorate to the point that it puts the success of the mission in doubt and his teammates' lives at risk.

Members of special operations units are like the members of a typical sports team in that they like to joke with their teammates, engage in various forms of horseplay and generally have a good time. And like the most successful sports teams, when it is *"game time,"* these men become focused to a degree that most people will never experience. It is this ability that separates special operators from most conventional soldiers, and likely one of the major differences between good athletes and great athletes.

Distractions of various types are the main impediment to proper focus and concentration. This topic – distractions and how to deal with them – have already been discussed in a previous chapter. Over time, highly successful athletes develop specific and tailored routines that help them avoid being distracted during situations where the need for intense focus and concentration is high.

You probably have already established specific routines for the phases of time leading up to the actual moment you begin competing in an event. You should reflect upon these routines and evaluate whether or not they are effective in enabling you to shut out distractions and enable you to focus on the event or contest you are about to engage in. Imagine how liberating and empowering it would be if your mind was able to focus solely on the event you are engaging in! This topic will be covered in greater detail in the *Before the Battle Begins* chapter.

Now that you are aware of some of the techniques used by SOF operators to control their natural reactions to the human stress response, it is important to remember that your body has been genetically *"hard wired,"* through millions of years of evolution, to react in certain ways to fear or threat stress. These physical responses never go away; they remain with us as long as we live. A special operator's ability to learn how to anticipate and control these predictable and ever-present responses is what enables him to keep a *"cool head"* in very dangerous situations and perform at optimal levels. As an athlete, this means that your body will also react predictably during times of high-stress, especially before and during important events where the stakes are high. You should experiment with the seven techniques discussed in this chapter and utilize them in a manner that best enhances your ability to cope with fear, stress, anxiety and any other physical and mental response you may experience while training and competing.

Breathing Technique

As mentioned in the previous chapter, one of the seven arousal-control techniques currently being taught to the men undergoing BUD/S is a breathing technique that is often referred to as *"4 x 4 breathing."* Simply stated, the 4 x 4 breathing technique is executed by inhaling deeply, as though you are trying to fill up your lungs, for four seconds, and then exhaling in a steady and even manner for four seconds. This sequence must be continuously repeated for at least one minute to be effective, and many advocates find that doing it for longer periods of two to six minutes produces even better results. I have utilized this technique countless times and know firsthand that it really works.

Medical research revealed that the 4 x 4 breathing technique essentially tricks the human brain into replicating certain calming and stress-reduction aspects associated with deep *rapid eye movement* (REM) phase of a person's nightly sleep pattern. The REM phase is the period of sleep that provides the most benefit from a rest and recuperation perspective. Obviously, if an individual is able to replicate some of the beneficial aspects of the REM phase during the day, while experiencing challenging and stressful situations, he or she would be better able to control certain aspects of the human stress response.

According to a medical doctor that works in the Naval Special Warfare community, BUD/S students use this breathing technique on a daily basis as they prepare for training evolutions such as timed distance runs and open-ocean swims, while waiting to begin a run of the obstacle course, or prior to jumping into the pool for a *"drown-proofing"* session. This doctor believes that most of these students continue to use this arousal-control technique after they graduate from BUD/S and go on to serve as members of an operational SEAL unit.

Methods such as the 4 x 4 breathing technique have literally been used for thousands of years, often combined with the use of meditation and other practices designed to enhance a person's focus and state of awareness. The use of breathing techniques is not unique to the SEAL community; members of other SOF units also utilize them, though the degree of formal training and adoption varies among these units. I will say that whenever I discussed the issue of remaining calm and focused during stressful situations with special operators of all ages and from various SOF units, all of them mentioned the use of breathing techniques. You should consider adopting this technique during your training, pre-competition routines and while engaging in actual competitions.

After you are done reading this chapter, put the book down and try the 4 x 4 breathing technique for a minute or two. If you consciously focus your attention on breathing in the manner described earlier, you'll start to notice several things start to happen, your heart rate might decrease, your awareness of your surroundings (sounds, temperature, etc.) may sharpen and you will likely feel yourself begin to relax. This technique requires a bit of practice, but an individual can gain mastery of it very quickly, within only a few days if it is performed correctly. I urge you to do this, because I think the use of the 4 x 4 breathing technique as a way to control arousal relative to the human stress response can literally be the difference between an athlete winning and losing high-stakes competitions.

Thinking without Limits

Most people, young and old, live their lives according to a predetermined perception of *"limitations."* It is human nature to always try to find the easiest way of doing something, to avoid any amount of physical discomfort or psychological stress. As such, it becomes quite easy for us to adopt a mindset that essentially prevents us from stepping out of our own self-imposed limitations, to step out of our comfort zone. We become satisfied with what we are doing and how we are doing it, mostly because we have been taught to believe that we are doing as much as is humanly possible or acceptable by the standards of our families, professions, the sports we participate in and the people that we typically socialize with.

This chapter is designed to cause you to reflect upon the mindset of high-achievers – individuals that went above and beyond what their peers, parents, coaches and teachers taught them was possible or acceptable. If you gain only one bit of wisdom from this chapter, let it be that every high-achiever reached that status simply because they chose to defy existing boundaries or limits associated with their particular field.

They simply decided that their dream was reachable if they focused all of their will and energy toward achieving it. They had to ignore the many individuals that were constantly telling them that what they were attempting was *"impossible."*

The concept of pushing past limitations permeates the entire special operations community. The infamous Navy SEAL BUD/S training and selection course was initially based on the assumption that men are physically capable of accomplishing at least 10 times that which is typically accepted as being the *"maximum capacity"* of the human body. As a result of this training, the SEAL teams are comprised of men who have proven to themselves and their teammates that they are capable of enduring what most men cannot. A closer look at the selection courses for other SOF units reveals the same type of rigor and evaluation based on the assumption that humans are capable of doing and enduring far more than they have been taught to believe since they were young children. SOF units in particular need individuals that can demonstrate the ability to break through these pre-conceived psychological and physical barriers and achieve and endure that which most men simply cannot bring themselves to do.

Much of what special operators do on a daily basis is very dangerous and well beyond the accepted limits of the human body's capability, yet they have mastered the art of making the difficult look easy. Obviously, the ability to push past accepted limits and norms is very important while trying to survive a selection course and serve in a SOF unit. I think most would agree that this ability is also an essential ingredient to high achievement as an athlete. To further illustrate the concept of *"no limits thinking"* and pushing past accepted boundaries, I want to introduce you to a story that doesn't get much attention these days, but is a prime example of what a motivated person can do when facing a challenge that most think is beyond attainment:

He Did What They Said Was Impossible!

During the first several decades of the 1900s, it was generally believed among doctors, scientists and athletes that it was literally impossible for a human to run a mile in less than four minutes. Many people believed that attempting to achieve this feat would result in serious harm to the runner, and some thought it could prove fatal to anyone foolish enough to push their body to such extremes.

An English runner, Roger Bannister, had initially accepted the conventional belief that a sub-four minute mile was impossible. Then, he broke the record for the 1500 meter run (a mile is 1600 meters). This feat planted a seed that led him to believe that he could also set a new record in the mile. His newly found belief and confidence made all of the difference; and on May 6th, 1954, Roger set a new world record, running the mile in 3 minutes and 59.4 seconds – he stunned the world by achieving the impossible!

Roger's accomplishment brought the young medical student quite a bit of fame and eventually, a Knighthood bestowed upon him by the Queen of England. His sub-four minute mile served another purpose; it showed others that it could be done. Encouraged by Roger's spectacular feat, runners around the world sharpened their focus and approach to the mile-run and here's what happened:

- 46 days later, Australia's Jim Landry broke the record again, running the mile in 3:58.

- Several weeks later Bannister and Landry both broke four minutes in the same race.

- During the next 30 years the world record for the mile has been broken 16 times.

- The record now stands at 3 minutes and 43 seconds and is held by Hicham El Guerrouj, a member of the Moroccan Olympic team.

- Since then thousands of people have run the mile in under four minutes.

- Many high school students have run sub-four minute miles.

- In 1997, Kenya's Daniel Komen ran TWO miles in LESS THAN EIGHT MINUTES!

Obviously, once Roger Bannister proved that the impossible was indeed possible, many others followed suit; because they now knew that while difficult, running a sub-4 minute mile was indeed attainable. Whatever your athletic goals are, chances are that someone has already achieved them. Unlike Roger Bannister, you can easily find many of these individuals by reading about your sport or talking with your coaches and you can use them as role models. This is comforting and encouraging at the same time, knowing that others have achieved what you aspire to. The truth is that they did it and you can too!

Lessons We Can Learn from Bannister's Accomplishment

Need for Support

Bannister actually had a lot of help before and during his historic run. He received a great deal of coaching on the technical aspects of world-class running and he could count on friends and family for logistical support. If you look at the video of his record-setting run, you'll see that a few teammates served as pace-setters to help him maintain the tempo required to break the four minute mark. Whatever it is that you desire to achieve as an athlete, chances are that you are going to need the help of others. Aside from the obvious benefit of receiving such support, it is very beneficial to surround yourself with other people who are also high-achievers that can encourage you as you push yourself toward achieving your goals.

Ignoring Critics

As stated earlier, at that time, the concept of a human running a sub-four minute mile had long been deemed impossible. When Bannister announced that he intended to achieve this, he was immediately met with criticism and ridicule. At the time, he was a medical student and some actually questioned his intelligence and psychological fitness for serving as a physician – they thought he was crazy! Although it took an immense amount of moral courage, he shrugged off all criticism of his pursuit of the impossible, and also weathered the fury of the British track and field establishment, which was highly critical of Bannister's training regimen. Even worse, despite the fact that what he was attempting was thought to be unattainable, these *"experts"* still expected him to train in a manner they thought *"appropriate!"* Bannister stood firm in the face of this criticism and trained as he deemed necessary. He ignored those who would tell him he was chasing an impossible dream and simply went out and proved them all wrong!

Special operations units are full of guys who were told, *"you'll never make it"* when they stated their desire to serve in elite units. Rather than accepting the fate that others had determined for them, they ignored their critics, passed selection and eventually became special operators. As an athlete, you will likely face similar critics and naysayers when you state your goals. Perhaps even those closest to you will doubt your ability to achieve your goal. If you listen to these people and buy into their negative thinking, you will be giving up on yourself.

Pushing through Pain

Most significant achievements require one to sacrifice, endure and push through challenging times. Obviously, for Bannister, his athletic feat (and the training prior to it) was accompanied by a high level of physical pain. If you've ever run at the limits of your own physical ability, you know that once you reach *"full throttle"* for an extended period of time your entire body feels as if it's on fire! It takes a strong will to push past this level of pain and discomfort. Bannister once said:

> *"The man who can drive himself further once the effort gets painful is the man who will win."*

Bannister's statement is completely aligned with the philosophies shared by the members of SOF units. For almost all athletes, there are often significant levels of physical, emotional and psychological stress associated with the pursuit of high achievement. These challenges will typically require young men and women to step outside their comfort zones and exceed limits they once thought daunting or nearly impossible. Doing so is often the difference between success and failure!

Ignoring Existing Barriers, Boundaries and Limits

In the case of the sub-four minute mile, it was deemed physically impossible. Many excellent runners did not even attempt to break this record because they thought trying to do so was simply a painful waste of time. Bannister showed that while difficult, it was indeed possible. There are countless other examples of athletes doing something that was thought to be outside the limits of human endurance or physical strength. You are probably aware of some examples of this within your particular sport, and I'm sure that your coaches can tell you many stories of athletes that defied all odds and achieved things far above what most thought he or she was capable of.

The main lesson is that high-achievers approach all barriers, boundaries and limitations as being artificial and man-made. They have the ability to believe in themselves and their dreams, even when all others ridicule them or try to convince them that *"it can't be done."* There's an old saying that applies here: *"If you can conceive it, you can achieve it!"*

Traits of High-Achievers

If you were able to study the psychological profiles of people who have achieved great success, you'd easily see patterns of thought and behavior that emerge as common denominators amongst them. Whether they are athletes, scientists, inventors or the special operators that are the focus of this book, they have all demonstrated the ability to push through barriers and limitations that others deemed insurmountable. In some instances, such as Roger Bannister's record-breaking run, they achieved things that rational people truly believed were beyond the reach of human beings. Many of these high-achievers were of average intelligence and more than a few had performed badly in traditional academic environments. Many had little or no formal training in areas in which they later became quite successful. In some instances, they were deemed *"losers"* by their families and friends. Obviously they weren't losers – far from it!

Here's something else they were not – conformists. Instead of conforming to the conventional wisdom and limitations that others allowed themselves to be constrained by, these people simply went about achieving that which the *"experts"* would not even attempt to do! Unfortunately, most people do conform to the limitations and boundaries created by others. They don't realize that they are allowing the thoughts and beliefs of others to limit their own thinking, and in the process, their level of success and achievement in many aspects of life!

Self-limiting Behavior

It is time for you to ask yourself some tough questions relative to your approach to your role as an athlete. Do you in various ways limit your ability to aspire to high-achievement or to dream lofty goals in your particular sport? Are you in the habit of telling yourself that something you'd like to achieve or do is too difficult or that you aren't capable of making it happen? Are you prone to making excuses for yourself whenever you begin to contemplate what you'd like to achieve as an athlete?

If you're like most young athletes, you probably have done all of the above at some point. This type of thinking is often referred to as *self-limiting behavior;* and it is the product of a person being restricted from making progress due to their own fears, unrealistic expectations and lack of confidence in his or her ability to succeed. The effects of self-limiting behavior range from slightly diminished personal or professional achievement (and happiness!) to significant or even complete failure.

Dave, a former member of one of the more secretive SOF units told me that prior to the start of his selection course, the senior member of the training cadre told the class:

> *"Alright men, it's time to get after it. You already know that most of the men attempting selection don't make it through the course successfully. I'm telling you the truth when I say that all of you have what it takes to pass selection, it's simply a matter of desire and how much physical pain you are willing to endure. Just remember that what you want is waiting for you on the other side of your fears. Good luck!"*

He went on to say that from that point forward, the members of the training cadre said very little to him and his fellow students; no words of encouragement or criticism. The students were also instructed not to speak with or otherwise communicate with anyone other than members of the training cadre. It was apparent to him that by design, the men going through selection were purposely being isolated, to the extent possible, into their own *"bubble"* so they had only their own thoughts to rely on during the very difficult evolutions that were part of the course.

The men that attempt this selection course must have a high level of mental toughness and self-confidence if they hope to make the grade.

215

I've never had an opportunity to speak with anyone that failed this particular selection course, but if I did, I'm sure that if they were honest with me, most of them would admit that at some point during the course, they simply gave in to their negative thoughts – the inner critic that told them, *"you can't do this"* or *"you're not good enough to pass selection."* As in many situations in life, negative thoughts, if not controlled or negated, often lead to self-limiting behavior.

In the case of men that failed this, or any other SOF selection course, for that matter, self-limiting behavior typically leads them to slow down during a graded event such as a timed run or swim; they begin to hold back from giving all of their energies to the task at hand and in many instances, they begin to lag behind their peers. Something inside their minds tells them *"it's no use, why bother when you know you're going to fail?"* or other negative thoughts. This typically leads to them not achieving a passing score on an event, and while all of the SOF selection courses are different from a curriculum perspective, the fact is that in all of them, a certain amount of failure will result in a student being dropped from the course.

Aside from those that are withdrawn from selection courses for failing to meet physical or academic standards, there are many students that simply quit. For some reason, they have lost the confidence and desire they had for joining a SOF unit. They were unable to understand what had been told to members of Dave's selection class, *"Just remember that what you want is waiting for you on the other side of your fears."* Remember, self-limiting behavior is almost always caused by self-limiting thinking!

Many psychologists agree that a great amount of a person's self-limiting behavior can be traced to his or her experiences as a child, perhaps how they were treated and raised by parents. Siblings and peers often have a major impact on how people begin to feel about themselves at a very early age, and in many instances, the attitude and level of *"self-worth"* developed in childhood carries on into adulthood.

One thing I have noticed amongst the members of SOF units that I worked with is that a majority of them apparently were very confident and focused as children and began showing signs of high levels of self-discipline and resiliency very early on in their lives. It is common to hear stories of these warriors demonstrating a strong will and *"fire in the gut"* when they were growing up, as young athletes and in social or academic settings.

In other words, many of today's special operators were once children and young adults who had a very strong belief in their ability to persevere and achieve things that many of their peers thought too difficult. If you were able to speak with the high school and college classmates, teachers and coaches of men currently serving in the SOF units, you'd invariably come away with the impression that these people were not surprised to see these men volunteer for, and complete the training required to become a special operator. Adjectives such as *"dedicated, focused, strong-willed and confident"* would inevitably surface in these conversations.

You should reflect upon what you've just read and contemplate what people will say about you in future years. Will they remember you as a dedicated and fierce competitor – a student of your sport - or as one that never really did what was necessary to become the very best athlete possible? Be honest with yourself and if you aren't satisfied with your current state as an athlete, make the decision to do whatever it takes to maximize your athletic potential!

Almost every special operator that I spoke with while doing research for this book said they knew one or more teammates from their previous conventional unit that, in their opinion, were absolutely capable of passing selection and becoming a member of their particular SOF unit. Yet, almost none of these men would volunteer for selection, even though in many cases they had previously expressed great interest in doing so. In fact, some of these men had actually engaged in extensive physical training in their off-duty time, in some instances for several years, in order to prepare themselves for the rigors of selection. When I asked them why they thought these men could not bring themselves to attempt selection, the operators typically felt that these men were simply afraid to risk failure, especially knowing that the majority of men attempting the selection course in the past had failed. Even though these men were physically capable of passing, and in some instances more physically gifted than their buddies that volunteered for and passed selection, they had apparently talked themselves into believing they could not pass the course and they remained in their conventional military units. These men are examples of what can happen when individuals engage in self-limiting behavior; untapped potential, failure to achieve personal or professional goals and almost certainly, disappointment and regret.

No Limits!

Even if you are not a fan of basketball, you likely know that in order to play this sport professionally, one has to be tall, much taller in fact, than the average human. It is a fact that the average height of the members of all the teams in the National Basketball Association is 6'7" and many of them weigh nearly 300 lbs. These guys are literally giants among men in a physical sense! Most people would readily accept that men under 6 feet tall would have little chance of obtaining a spot on an NBA team roster, yet it has been done! In a sport dominated by giants, players like Spud Webb (5'7"), Muggsy Bogues (5'3") and Earl Boykins (5'5") not only competed, but they performed at a higher level of success than many of their taller opponents! While these individuals are extreme examples of unusually short men making the grade as professional basketball players, there have been many players under 6' tall that have prospered in the NBA. How is this possible? The answer is obvious – all along they were thinking without limits – they all believed in their ability to play in the NBA and they simply went out and made it happen!

Here's another story associated with thinking without limits that you may not have heard before. In 1939, a University of California–Berkeley graduate student named George Dantzig was 15 minutes late to one of his advanced mathematics classes. Prior to his arrival, the professor had written two famous examples of *"unsolvable"* statistics problems on the blackboard and briefly discussed them with the students. When he sat down, Dantzig saw the problems on the blackboard, assumed they were homework assignments and wrote them down. Later in the week, he handed in his homework to the professor and went about his daily routine.

A few days later, Dantzig was awakened by his professor banging on his door at 6am. When he opened his door he heard the professor exclaim, *"You did it! You solved the problems that nobody else could solve!"* George Dantzig had indeed solved two statistical problems that had been deemed *"unsolvable"* by the world-wide science and mathematics communities for many decades. When asked about the problems, Dantzig admitted that they had seemed *"more difficult than the typical homework assigned by the professor"*, but he simply kept working on them for a few days until he arrived at a solution for both of them.

This is an instance in which a person wasn't even aware that what he was attempting to do was *"impossible."* Because Dantzig didn't know these problems *"couldn't be solved"* he approached them with confidence, knowing that his professor's homework assignments, while often difficult, were always solvable. Dantzig solved the problems because he didn't know he couldn't! This is a great example of thinking without limits and how much a person can accomplish if he or she isn't constrained by established or implied boundaries, limitations or *"impossible"* situations.

Another example of what thinking-without-limits can do for a person is the story of distance-swimmer Diana Nyad. When she was 29 years old, she set a goal for herself to swim from Cuba to Key West, Florida. Her first attempt at this feat, in 1978, failed as did three subsequent attempts over the next 30 years. Finally, on September 2, 2013, at the age of 64, after swimming more than 100 miles in shark-infested waters, Diana achieved her long time goal. After her 53-hour ordeal was over, she told reporters:

> *"I got three messages. One is we should never, ever give up. Two is you never are too old to chase your dreams. Three is it looks like a solitary sport, but it's a team effort."*

Yet one more story that shows what not limiting our thinking can do is one that happened some years ago. A highly regarded Navy SEAL officer was injured in a training accident and, as a result, lost the lower portion of one of his legs, starting about 3 inches below the knee joint. At the time, medical science and prosthetic limbs were not as advanced as they are today, and this young officer's injury was considered by doctors and senior SEAL leaders to be one that rendered him incapable of continued service as a SEAL. When the mention of being medically retired began surfacing in conversations with doctors and his SEAL leaders, this officer politely and defiantly declared that he intended to recover from his injury and return to his unit as an operator. He assured anyone who'd listen to him that all he wanted was the opportunity to recover from the injury and regain the ability to meet the physical standards of being a SEAL.

I don't think anyone involved in this situation doubted the young officer's desire to return to his unit. But, I'd say that nearly all of them simply couldn't fathom a man missing the lower part of his leg, even one who'd already served as a fully qualified SEAL, would be able to regain the ability to meet the physical standards associated with being an operator. To make a long story short, this officer not only made it back to his unit as a fully capable SEAL, but he went on to become a highly accomplished senior officer and commander within the Naval Special Warfare community.

There are countless stories of high-achievers, like the SEAL officer mentioned above, who have achieved great things mainly because they believed they could. These people know that within each person - including you - is a reservoir of untapped potential and capability that is waiting to be used. All that is needed to unleash this *"secret weapon"* is the decision to use it. Once you decide that it is time to stretch yourself and go past boundaries and limits that previously stopped you, there's literally no limit to what you can achieve!

What's Your Four-Minute Mile?

Is there something you want to achieve or do as an athlete that everyone else thinks is impossible, like Roger Bannister's critics did when he announced his goal of running a sub-four minute mile? Is your goal or dream something that perhaps even you think is unattainable? Maybe you've actually started pursuing this goal and gave up when faced with difficulties? Perhaps you made an attempt and failed? Your four-minute mile might even be something that many others have accomplished, it just seems unattainable or *"too hard"* for you.

All of these negative thoughts are just limitations that your mind has created. In order to succeed, you must start believing you can win – it is really as simple as that. Whatever it is that you want to achieve, the first step to achieving it is to convince yourself that while it may be difficult, you can do it! It is this self-belief that enables you to ignore the critics and do whatever it takes to reach your goal.

If you were able to speak with career special operators, men that had served in SOF units for twenty or more years, all of them would tell you that practically everything of significance they had achieved during their career had once seemed quite daunting or even impossible to them. But, they dismissed their own negative thoughts and, in many instances, those of their critics, and faced the challenges associated with their goals head-on, with every bit of energy and focus they possessed. Over time, as they had amassed one significant accomplishment after another, these warriors came to understand that just about anything of high value in this life is typically associated with great challenges seemingly impossible to overcome. Yet, they learned that in most instances, what often seems at first glance to be impossible is actually quite possible, as long as a person simply decides to dedicate his or her efforts to doing whatever it takes to achieve success. You will find this out for yourself the moment you decide to pursue your goals with every ounce of will power, energy and enthusiasm that you possess!

Before the Battle Begins

One of your goals as an athlete must be to train your mind so that, whether in practice or in actual competition, you are mentally tough and always prepared to perform with a high degree of focus. You've probably heard your coaches' state that *"you will play as you practice."* This is an accurate statement and it should make you realize that your performance during competition is always a direct reflection of your performance during your training and pre-event preparation.

This chapter is specifically focused on some tactics and techniques that you can use to prepare yourself just before a competitive event. That said, you need to understand that effective pre-event preparation will not overcome prior laziness in practice or other aspects of inadequate or improper training and conditioning. But, for an athlete that has indeed *"done the work,"* the knowledge that he or she has worked hard in practice, both during the season and the off-season, will greatly influence their self-confidence and will contribute greatly to effective pre-competition mental preparation.

225

Mental Preparation

As mentioned previously, being mentally prepared for a competition should be the goal of every athlete. While most athletes understand the importance of physically warming up right before an event, fewer understand how critical it is to conduct an effective *"mental warm up."* Those who do understand this, know that not only does the body need to be warmed up, (muscles ready to exert force, heart rate elevated to get the blood pumping, etc.), but the mind also needs to get fully prepared to *"go to war."* At this point in the book, you probably agree with the assertion that when all else is equal among two athletes at the beginning of a contest, the one who is most mentally prepared to *"leave everything on the field"* is usually the athlete that wins.

In addition to my extensive military service, I've been associated with sports for many years as an athlete, coach and a parent of athletes. I can state without reservation that many of the athletes I observe at the youth, high school and college levels, often sabotage themselves with ineffective or even damaging pre-competition preparation. Many of them focus too much on the various negative thoughts related to fear of failure, and are already worried about what their coaches, their dad, brother, teammates and friends will say to them or think about them if they lose the contest. In other words, at the time when they are supposed to be thinking positive thoughts focused on winning the game or match that is about to begin, they are already preparing to deal with the aftermath of losing it!

You don't need to be a psychologist to understand that if a person's mind is focused on *"damage control"* – how they're going to deal with losing a contest - it cannot focus on winning it! This diversion of focus from the task at hand leaves the athlete unprepared mentally to perform at the peak of his or her athletic potential.

If you speak with any athlete who has upset a top ranked or *"big name"* opponent, they will almost always tell you that they began the contest knowing that they could win; that they had mentally prepared by focusing on exerting all of their energy and skill during the event. In other words, they believed they could win (even if others did not!) and they psyched themselves up to the point where they had promised themselves that win or lose – they were going to *"let it all out"* and play hard throughout the entire contest. Often, athletes that do this and are mentally *"prepared for combat"* right from the start of the competition are able to catch more accomplished competitors off-guard; this is one reason there will always be *"upsets"* in the world of sports. Remember, the best athlete doesn't always win the contest, the one that *"competes the best"* during the contest does!

The Five Major Causes of Pre-Competition Anxiety

I could write volumes on the various pre-competition mental challenges that athletes have to deal with, but I think I've written enough to get you to understand that without proper focus and pre-competition preparation, you can sabotage your chances of winning. By training your mind to focus on positive self-talk, visualization and other techniques you've learned about in previous chapters and by following the game plan your coach has discussed with you, you can obtain a mindset that makes you determined to *"leave everything on the field"* during an upcoming event.

1. During the many years I have spent observing athletes at all levels, I have narrowed the sources of pre-competition anxiety to four major factors:

2. They fail to "lock down" their mind. Often athletes are thinking about or even discussing with their friends and family about what they are going to do or where they are going to eat after the event or tournament. They become distracted by talking and thinking about social events and other things that are totally unrelated to the task at hand: winning the contest that is about to start!

3. They fear failure. Athletes focused on the negatives associated with losing a competition are practically guaranteeing that they will lose!

4. Excessive worry about what others will think of them. Instead of being focused on winning an upcoming event, athletes too often have great anxiety about what other people will think about them if they lose or don't perform well. These athletes will tell you that they often find themselves thinking about this while competing!

5. They lack confidence. This is very common and I think it is because all athletes truly know whether they have done

everything they could have done prior to an event to prepare physically, technically and mentally. In other words, if an athlete knows he's been taking shortcuts in practice and hasn't worked hard during conditioning, this will usually cause self-doubt. Before long the mind starts making excuses or reasons why winning is unlikely or even impossible.

If you identify with any of these pre-competition challenges, you can benefit from more structured and focused mental preparations. Obviously, the time period after your arrival at the venue is a good time to mentally prepare yourself for combat and eliminate doubt, anxiety, tension, and at the same time elevate your confidence, composure, and trust in your technique and knowledge of *"what needs to be done"* once you walk out onto the arena floor or playing field.

The Five Steps to Effective Pre-Competition Mental Preparation

Below is a list of five steps for effective pre-competition mental preparation. Realize that each athlete is somewhat unique and based on personality and maturity level; these five steps can be modified to fit the needs of any individual.

1. **Eliminate Pressure by Managing Expectations:** Many athletes harm their chances of winning by setting expectations that are unrealistic or unnecessary. Often, athletes focus on scoring a certain number of points against their opponent instead of simply focusing on winning the event. If you focus on winning, it enables you to be more flexible-minded during a contest and

"find ways to win" instead of focusing on winning in a certain way or by using certain techniques.

2. **Give Yourself Reasons for Being Confident:** If you have listened to your coaches, put in the requisite off-season work, trained hard during the season and sharpened your technical skills, you can reflect on this during the pre-competition period. Reflecting on your previous preparation and sacrifices will bolster your confidence as you realize that you have indeed done everything possible to prepare to win the upcoming event. Knowing that you've done everything your coaches have asked you to do and that you've sacrificed to arrive at your current level of fitness and technical soundness is very powerful and will enable you *"to believe in yourself"* when you are psyching yourself up prior to an event.

3. **Focus on The Event:** If you can *"put a fence around your mind"* and focus solely on the upcoming event, your chances of winning increase greatly. Instead of focusing on outside distractions, you must be able to *"lock down"* your mind and allow only thoughts of success in the competition. The best athletes will tell you that they never think about anything else prior to a contest, but the contest itself and what they need to do to win it. This is especially true in tournament situations, when athletes are often thinking of who they are going to have to face in the finals, and they lose sight of the fact that they actually have to win their early matches or games to get into the semi-finals and finals! Never look past your next game or match and do not allow

yourself to have any thoughts about anything not related to that contest.

4. **Have Confidence in Your Training:** As you prepare for the upcoming competition, it is very beneficial to reflect on your training and all that you've done up to this point. Knowing you have truly put in the time and effort to excel at your sport is a huge motivator when mentally preparing for an event. It breeds confidence and allows an athlete to reflect on all of his or her past work and sacrifice; and to realize that he or she is indeed well prepared and ready to compete at a high level during the upcoming event.

5. **Expect Tension and Deal with It Effectively:** The pre-competition period can be stressful for an athlete. Any athlete who claims that he or she feels no amount of apprehension, nervousness or *"jitters"* prior to an event is either not telling the truth, or he or she doesn't realize that they are actually experiencing stress. Humans experience physiological, mental and emotional responses when readying to enter a battle, fight or conflict. In other words, if you are properly preparing for a competition, adrenaline levels will be elevated as part of the human stress response, which may cause you to feel somewhat *"jittery"* or nervous, incapable of sitting still and even thirsty. Know that these reactions (and several others) are typical and can be expected prior to any competitive event.

How to Deal With Pre-Competition Tension

The human stress response is predictable and it is unfailingly present every time you sense some type of imminent danger or stressful event. As discussed in a previous chapter, these physiological responses that your body experiences typically cause elevated heart rates, jitters, dry mouth, etc. These responses are normal and they are also unavoidable. This is the *SCIENCE* associated with pre-game tension or jitters. The *ART* of dealing with these predictable physiological reactions lies on your ability to cope with them and even turn them into an asset. This will allow you to begin any competition with a fully engaged, highly focused *"warrior's mindset"* that has shut out all distractions and is focused on nothing more than the battle that is about to begin.

Of course, some of the physical reactions your body has toward pending combat – elevated heart rate and blood pressure, sweating, increased thirst, frequent need to urinate and tense muscles, can produce negative effects on an athlete's pre-competition state of mind if he or she allows them to do so. Along with these physical reactions come predictable mental reactions, such as dwelling on fear of losing, feeling that you are not fully prepared for the competition, fear of embarrassing yourself in front or your family, girlfriend, boyfriend, coaches, teammates,

There are, however, positives that you can gain from the pre-competition tension that you feel. Obviously, you want to develop the ability to focus on these positive aspects and turn them into a weapon that enables you to think only good things about competing, the contest ahead of you, your prior training and conditioning and everything else that will allow you to *"talk to yourself"* and reflect on how well prepared you are for this event and how you have every reason to expect to do well on this day.

If you are truly a competitor, an impending competition will mean that you will soon become a *"gladiator"* doing battle in an arena before hundreds or thousands of fans. This elation will undoubtedly prompt positive thoughts and you'll view the upcoming event in a very positive way. Anticipating that your teammates, many of whom you've known for a long time, will be right beside you, makes the entire competition even more appealing to many athletes. Performing in front of family and friends is yet another motivating factor that many athletes use to psyche themselves up prior to a competition. They view the opportunity to perform in front of a crowd in a very positive light and this helps them elevate their game. All of these factors, and many more, can help an athlete become highly focused on the positive aspects of the event that is about to begin.

I have talked with many top-level athletes and they all say that during pre-game mental preparation against the very best opponents in their respective sports, they reflect on how much they've done to get to this point...the sacrifices that they've made...the years of training and preparation they've put in...how they are fully equipped to beat their opponent... and that...THEY DESERVE TO WIN...and will do so if they focus on...GIVING IT THEIR ALL DURING EVERY SECOND OF THE EVENT!

This thought process leads these athletes to enter a competition against top ranked opponents...EXPECTING TO WIN and...REFUSING TO ACCEPT ANYTHING LESS THAN 100% EFFORT FROM THEMSELVES!

The 5 Things That Nearly All Champion Athletes Do Prior to an Event

Almost all the professional and world class amateur athletes I have had opportunity to observe execute the following actions in some form or another. Learning what these high achievers do can be very beneficial to you and these techniques can be effective at every level of sport.

1. **They insulate themselves from distractions:** These athletes often cut off all contact with parents, friends and significant others a couple of hours prior to an event. They often isolate themselves in a different part of the arena or gym and avoid socializing and anything else that distracts them from thinking only about their upcoming event. This enables them to entirely focus on their performance without having to respond to questions or participate in conversations with others. This is a superb technique and I recommend that you find some variation of it for your pre-competition routine.

2. **They listen to music to calm their nerves and get inspired:** One NCAA wrestling champion told me that he listened to selected songs from the soundtrack of the movie *"Gladiator"* because he

234

viewed himself as a modern-day gladiator and the music inspired him. He also told me that as he ran into the arena toward the elevated mat for his NCAA finals match, he imagined that he was in Rome running into the famed Coliseum in front of thousands of fans. Like the ancient gladiators who knew they had to win to survive, he convinced himself that he was in a battle for survival and that he had to wrestle his finals match as if his life depended upon him winning it. He did win his finals match – against an opponent who had previously beaten him during the regular season. So, find some music that calms you, inspires you and *"insulates"* you from distractions during your pre-competition mental preparation.

3. **They have a set pre-competition routine:** The most successful competitors have an established routine they follow beginning at the moment they arrive at the venue where the event will be played until they actually begin competing. Many eat the same type of food and drink the same fluids – knowing that their body has responded well to this in the past and that they won't feel sluggish or bloated while warming up or competing. They also have a set routine for physically warming up – often performing specific exercises and stretches in a set sequence, duration, number of reps, etc. Some also use a drilling partner they have become used to and they execute a prescribed number of selected drills, moves, techniques, etc., during their warm up.

4. **They start the event fully warmed up:** A proper warm-up should result in elevated heart rate and a light sweat. If you've ever watched a professional boxing match or mixed martial arts fight,

you'll notice that all of the competitors enter the ring or cage already sweating prior to the start of the event. This enables them to be physically ready to engage in the flurries and scrambles that often occur right from the start of the fight. In other words, they realize that they need to be ready to go full force against an opponent, and they won't have time to warm up during the first few rounds of the fight! Take a lesson from these competitors, both professional and amateur – the very best athletes ALWAYS have a pre-game warm up that leaves them fully warmed up and sweating. This produces a body that is ready to face any threat thrown at it during the early stages of a game or match and it also provides a great deal of self-confidence to an athlete, knowing that should an *"ambush"* come his way at the onset of the event, his *"engine"* is fully warmed up and ready to operate at peak horsepower!

5. **They stay hydrated:** This is an often overlooked aspect of dealing with pre-competition tension and stress. Your body's instinctive reaction to the stress of an upcoming fight or competition will usually include greater frequency of urination, which will rob the body of necessary fluid. Additionally, the pre-game warm up, if done well, will result in some degree of sweating and this water must also be replaced. The worst thing you can do is start an event with reduced hydration levels. It is beyond doubt that a body that is lacking its *"full tank"* of water will inevitably fail or underperform during high level competition. This is especially true during tournament settings, where athletes will participate in several games or matches strung out over an 8-12 hour period.

It is easy to become dehydrated during these prolonged competitions and you should develop a system that requires you to drink at least one or two 12 ounce bottles of water per hour. Stay hydrated!

Performing Your Best When You Are Outmatched

Competitiveness is a quality that all champion athletes possess; they simply love to win and this drives them to succeed. However, a strong competitive drive can work against some athletes because even with the smallest of failures or setbacks, they lose confidence, become frustrated with themselves and lose motivation.

All top level athletes are driven to win and the mere thought of losing a competition is distasteful to them. These athletes are often fueled more by a hatred of losing than a love of winning. This can sometimes work against them when they are matched against opponents who are simply more skilled than they are. Often, when facing a top-tier opponent, athletes begin doubting their ability to win, especially if they have previously lost to the opponent or if the opponent is a *"big name"* competitor that has a reputation for being unbeatable. Many athletes can fall victim to self-doubt in such a situation and can literally *"talk themselves out of winning"* an event that they could win if they had been properly focused.

It is important that you remain focused on proper pre-competition mental preparation when you are about to battle an opponent that is more experienced and more proficient than you are. Rather than dwell on the fact that you are overmatched, you should home in on several thoughts that can slowly boost your confidence. If you can focus instead on a different strategy - avoiding being scored upon in the early stages of the event, or keeping within a certain number of points from your opponent at the halfway point of the game, etc. – you can convince yourself that there's a chance that you could pull off an upset. Whatever it is (scoring, not being scored upon, avoiding an opponent's better moves, etc.) that you and your coaches decide that you should focus on during the event, the fact is that if you get your mind believing that if you manage to do what your coaches are advising you to do – YOU WILL HAVE A CHANCE AT VICTORY!

Once you believe you can actually beat a superior opponent if certain things happen (or don't happen, in some situations) your entire approach to a competition becomes one that is focused on winning vice trying not to lose. Reflect on what I just wrote in the previous sentence – there is a huge difference in the mindset of an athlete who is *trying to win* and one who is *trying not to lose*. The athletes that pull off upsets when facing superior opponents were able to talk themselves into TAKING ACTION when opportunities appeared and they SCORED POINTS instead of waiting passively for the *"superior athlete"* to attempt an offensive move that would cause them to continually remain on the defensive and rob them of the *"attacker's advantage"*.

Here are some of the techniques used by top level athletes to mentally prepare for situations when they are facing the toughest opponents.

Acknowledge that you are "going to war:" You have to acknowledge that you are about to engage in a tough battle against a very skilled opponent and that by most criteria, you are not favored to win this battle. By accepting this mentally, you begin to overlook the fact that winning this competition will require you to perform at *"personal best"* levels of skill, strength, endurance and technique – and you will be able to better focus on what you actually have to execute from a strategy and tactics standpoint to defeat your opponent. Remember, if you think you have a chance at winning this contest, you do! So, get your mind wrapped around the fact that you're about to participate in the toughest event of your career to date, and that you're ready to throw everything you have physically and mentally at your opponent.

Have a Game Plan and Execute It: Talk to your coaches and seek their advice. They will probably know your opponent and his or her style of competing, favorite moves, etc. Together, devise a game plan, period by period, of what you need to do to avoid his or her strengths and maximize your chances at scoring points. Most coaches know what advice to provide to you and the best coaches will actually state which techniques you should focus on in order to deny the opponent the use of his favorite moves.

For example, I once observed a nationally famous high school wrestling coach talking to one of his wrestlers prior to his state finals match. His wrestler had lost to his finals opponent the previous week by a score of 10-2 and had been repeatedly taken down with double-leg shots. This coach advised his wrestler (Wrestler A) to tie up quickly with his opponent (Wrestler B), dig into underhooks and despite this being a folk-style match, he told his wrestler to:

> *"Wrestle only upper-body for the first period, as if you were in a Greco-Roman match. Keep him tied up defending your underhooks and don't let him get enough space to shoot his double leg."*

Wrestler A executed his coach's instructions and he frustrated his opponent by *"wrestling upper body"* and denying him the space he needed to get his double leg shot off. Frustrated by not being able to score on an opponent he'd easily taken down the week before, Wrestler B took a sloppy shot near the end of the first period and Wrestler A spun around him for a two point lead at buzzer. Wrestler A chose the neutral position at the start of the second period and continued to execute his coach's strategy. Once again Wrestler B could not avoid the constant pressure and crowding Wrestler A was putting on him and he attempted another sloppy double leg, which Wrestler A countered with a *"pancake,"* putting his opponent to his back, scoring a quick 5 points and ending the second period with a 7-0 lead.

240

At the start of the third period, Wrestler B was clearly panicked by the fact that he was losing badly to someone he'd easily beaten the week before. He chose the bottom position and Wrestler A, on the direction of his coach, released him in order to get back to the neutral position and once again, he wrestled *"upper body"* against his opponent. Distracted by the score and the fact that time was running out, Wrestler B also started trying to wrestle upper body in search of a big move that could put Wrestler A directly to his back.

With less than a minute to go in the match, he pushed hard into Wrestler A trying to dig his own underhooks and possibly get a bear hug on his opponent. Wrestler A was actually an accomplished upper-body wrestler and promptly headlocked Wrestler B to his back for five points and a 12-1 victory in the state finals!

Wrestler A wasn't supposed to win this match – but he went into it believing he could and he listened to his coach's advice. He whipped what many felt was a superior wrestler – BECAUSE HE HAD CONVINCED HIMSELF THAT HE COULD WIN THE MATCH!

Stick to The Plan: As described above, you should work with your coach and devise a strategy for an upcoming game or match. Review it with your coach to ensure that you fully understand it and mentally rehearse the strategy over and over until you know exactly what you are going to do once the event starts. Having a teammate drill the strategy with you is a perfect way to refine the strategy and also occupy your mind so it doesn't have time to dwell on negative thoughts. Once the whistle blows and the competition begins, you must remember to *"stick to the plan"* and keep battling for every second of every minute of the contest.

If you approach your training, your pre-competition preparation and your game plans and strategies with due diligence, having carefully gone through all the steps addressed in this chapter, there is no doubt in my mind that you will be better positioned for success during the battles that are in your future!

Setting Goals

The practice of setting goals is one of the most important things you can do in order to ensure you will achieve the results you desire. As mentioned earlier in this book, many special operators decided at a very young age that they were going to become a member of the Army's Special Forces, Air Force Pararescue, the 75th Ranger Regiment or other SOF unit. They began researching the specific unit they were interested in and learned about the various physical and academic requirements associated with joining the unit.

In most cases, these youngsters were not yet capable of meeting even the minimum physical standards required for getting the chance to apply for the opportunity to join a SOF unit. This meant that they had to set goals that, if achieved, would bring them up to satisfactory levels of strength and endurance. Those that were successful at achieving their goals used some method or technique to ensure they stayed on track and made the appropriate degree of progress at an appropriate pace.

Countless studies have revealed that the human brain is instinctively a goal-seeking organism. It is beyond debate that establishing goals and embedding them in the subconscious mind results in a more focused, determined and persistent individual. In other words, when you consciously reflect upon goals you want to achieve, write them down and review them on a daily basis, they begin to occupy a prominent position in your subconscious mind. This causes your mind to think of these goals on a continuous basis without the individual even knowing that it is happening.

Goal-Setting Systems

There are many proven goal-setting systems, methods and techniques that can be used to help you achieve your goals. Some are very simple and others quite sophisticated. You can find hundreds of books devoted to the topic of goal setting. Don't allow this to confuse you or to cause you anxiety about which system or method you should choose. The most important thing to focus on is that you must choose and utilize a goal-setting method or technique that works well for you. Without the use of some type of goal-setting system, your chances of achieving your dreams as an athlete will be greatly diminished.

One goal-setting system that is very popular among members of various special operations units is the SMART Goals System. It is a proven system and the one that I used throughout my military career; and I know for a fact that it is used by many special operators in their professional and personal lives. Additionally, my research on this topic has shown that this system is also used by many high-level amateur and professional athletes participating in various individual and team sports.

The SMART Goals System

This system involves five key elements: a goal that's specific, measurable, attainable, relevant and time-bound.

Specific Goals: This element stresses the need for specific and very detailed goals instead of more broadly defined, general ones. All goals must be clear and unambiguous, without unnecessary adjectives or vague statements. For goals to be specific, they must illustrate exactly what is expected, why is it important, who's involved, where is it going to happen and which attributes are important.

A specific goal will usually answer these questions:

- What: What is the desired end state?
- Why: Specific benefits of accomplishing the goal.
- Who: A list of people directly or indirectly involved in achieving the goal.
- Where: If appropriate to the situation, the locations associated with the goal.

Measurable Goals: All goals must be able to be clearly defined and measured. Goals that can be measured are more easily monitored for progress, need for modification of plans and timeliness. Experienced planners agree that the majority of people or organizations that fail to reach their goals do so because they did not apply an adequate form of measurement to keep track of their progress.

A measurable goal will usually answer questions such as:

- How much?

- How many?

- How will I know when the goal is achieved?

Attainable Goals: This book emphasizes the need for athletes to engage in *"no-limits thinking"* and *"stretching"* beyond real or perceived limitations to accomplish their goals. Most goals of a significant value are in fact *"stretch goals"* that require the mental toughness and resolve to push through barriers, but the fact remains that they must be attainable. Some athletes set goals that are too aggressive, to the point that they become unrealistic or unattainable.

An attainable goal will usually answer these questions:

- Have others already accomplished it?

- How can the goal be accomplished?

- Do you have access to the knowledge, tools and support required to accomplish it?

Relevant Goals: It is important to select goals that actually help you achieve your desired end state. A college swimmer's goal of completing a marathon in the off-season may be relevant to her personal life, but it will likely not have any impact on her chances of making the Olympic swimming team. This is a critical concept that you must understand completely! It is imperative that you write down a list of what you really want to achieve as an athlete and ensure that all other goals, objectives and efforts associated with your life are relevant to accomplishing the things on this list.

A relevant goal can answer yes to these questions:

- If I accomplish this, will my highest and most important goals be reached?

- Is this the right time to do this?

- Does accomplishing this goal enhance my chances of success toward accomplishing my ultimate end-state?

Time-bound Goals: All goals must be associated with specific dates of completion. Aligning a goal with specific dates and time-related milestones instills a sense of urgency and accountability among the people involved in accomplishing it. It also enables the measurement aspect of the SMART Goals Method, as previously discussed. Last, but not least, setting time parameters and due dates is very helpful in ensuring that the progress toward accomplishing a goal is not overtaken by the inevitable emergencies or issues that occur in everyone's lives. When such things happen, having a set timeline enables you to quickly assess how much your plan has been affected and can help you set a new course to regain momentum and get back on track.

A time-bound goal will usually answer these questions:

- When will the goal be achieved?

- What are the intermediate due dates assigned to micro-tasks or smaller objectives?

- What progress must be achieved by next week, six weeks from now, in 90 days?

- What specific actions am I taking today, this week, for the next 60 days, etc.?

The SMART Goal System has worked for many special operators and athletes alike, and it can work for you. I know that you have dreams and objectives that you want to accomplish as an athlete. Creating well-designed goals is the first step in making them happen!

It's Time for Action

Over the course of many years spent working with and observing members of SOF units, I have found that the one thing that separates the good, solid special operators from those that are recognized as being truly exceptional is that those in the latter group had a *bias for action* to a far greater degree than those in the former.

How did some special operators manage to rise above their highly-capable peers in various skills? In every instance that I am aware of, they achieved this by devoting time toward additional practice and study, sometimes doing so at their own expense. The lesson here is that even within SOF units, there are individuals who decide that they want to excel and exceed the standard levels of training. So, they take action, and whatever it is that they want to become more adept at or learn more about, they find ways to make it happen.

One example of this is found among the *"shooters"* that are found in most SOF units. These operators are the *"door kickers,"* the members of assault teams that actually enter buildings, caves, tunnels, ships and aircraft and other places that are often occupied by enemy forces. Every one of these men is very skilled in CQB and the standards for speed and accuracy places these men among the very best in the world at this skill. However, even among these groups of supremely confident warriors, there is an acknowledgement, often unspoken, that some operators are able to shoot at a superior level of speed and accuracy, and these men often become known as the *go-to-guys* during missions requiring split-second, precision shooting. In most instances, these operators do not possess any more natural ability relative to shooting than their peers do, but they often devoted a great amount of their off-duty time toward the refinement of various aspects of their shooting skills.

Another related example (which I alluded to in an earlier chapter) of the benefits of taking action occurred many years ago, when some of today's SOF units were still in their infancy. The leaders within these units knew their training cadre needed to acquire more advanced knowledge and training in the art and science of CQB. To accomplish this, selected unit members attended some civilian-operated shooting schools and they also trained with the highly-experienced SWAT units of several major cities. They also sought knowledge from some exceptionally capable foreign special operations units that had much experience in the field of counter-terrorist operations, especially assault-type operations that included various CQB techniques. Because they did this during the early stages of the integration of CQB skills into the mission profiles of their respective units, they were able to absorb and integrate some incredibly effective tactics and techniques that greatly elevated the effectiveness of the operators in these units, to the point where these units are now considered by many to be the *"Gold Standard"* when it comes to the science and art of CQB operations.

The main lesson I'm trying to convey through these examples is that whatever it is that you want to achieve as an athlete; <u>you must demonstrate a bias for action</u> in order to gain additional knowledge and become better at your sport. Even if things appear to be difficult and obstacles surface that might threaten your ability to take action, you must proceed, you must move forward and make things happen. Don't become a slave to planning, goal setting or other conceptual or administrative aspects associated with achieving the things you want to achieve, at some point you simply must get started on the path to success.

Action – Not Excuses!

Remember that it is a fundamental law of warfare that *"No battle plan survives the first shot,"* which means that even the best made plans have to be adjusted and modified once situations change. Assessments, setting goals and planning steps to achieve your athletic objectives are certainly important, but they will ultimately be useless unless you take action!

There's never a perfect time to take action. For most young athletes, there's always something going on that could easily be used as an excuse or reason why they can't take action. Don't fall into this trap. Do not join or remain in the legions of young athletes who are unsatisfied with their current level of achievement or who aspire to higher levels of achievement and success, only to sit idle because of excuses such as:

- Being a student takes up all of my time.

- I have to spend time with my family, girlfriend/boyfriend, friends, etc.

- Nobody else on my team has ever done this before.

- I'm not sure how my friends will react if I start devoting more time to my sport.

- I'm not ready to do this yet, but I will be next year.

Let's face it, successful athletes, those you admire and want to emulate, are in many ways very much like special operators. They are usually very action-oriented; they have a bias for action and are focused on making progress toward their goals. A bias for action does not mean you should act impulsively, rather, having a bias for action simply means you get things moving. This enables you to spend more time executing your plan and refining it as you move forward. As discussed in previous chapters, you must establish set goals, break them down into smaller micro-goals and try to anticipate obstacles and unforeseen issues that you must adapt to.

Victory Goes to the Risk Takers

All of this talk of taking action may be somewhat unnerving to many readers. This is understandable, because over many thousands of years, man has learned to seek safety and security; for most of us, our inclination is to avoid taking risks whenever possible. That said, the higher your goals are as an athlete, the more likely it is that you will have to step outside of your comfort zone and while doing so, expose yourself to various forms of risk.

There's nothing wrong with feeling anxious about, or perhaps even a bit scared of, the obstacles or risks that you may face as you strive to achieve your goals. Likewise, should you experience setbacks or unforeseen challenges as you pursue your goals, you should simply take time to reflect upon what you are trying to achieve and why it is so important to you. Remind yourself what kind of a person and athlete you are trying to become and visualize yourself performing well during important competitions. As discussed in previous chapters, engage in positive self-talk and temper any negative thoughts with thoughts of courage and self-reliance.

Very few great opportunities or high achievements in the world of sports come without risk, thus you should embrace it as something that is simply another challenge that must be recognized, assessed and overcome with persistence and skill. You can achieve your goals, despite any risk that may be associated with them; the key is courage, mental toughness and laser-like focus.

Conclusion

As a result of reading this book, you've been exposed to many different concepts, philosophies and techniques that are used by members of SOF units to consistently perform at levels of excellence that few can match. I urge you to reflect upon the kind of person and athlete you are at this time and the kind you would like to be in the future. Once you know what your goals are, seek the advice of your coaches, parents and mentors regarding the creation of a realistic plan to achieve them. Above all, it is critical that you understand that whatever your personal situation is, and no matter what sport you are participating in, nothing will change unless you take action!

GOOD LUCK!